I Am Not Just a Teacher

by

Robert J. Denise

PAGE PUBLISHING, INC.
New York, NY

First originally published by Page Publishing, Inc. 2014

ISBN 978-1-63417-556-2 (pbk)
ISBN 978-1-63417-557-9 (digital)

Printed in the United States of America

Foreword

The inspiration for writing this piece of prose came to me while I was attending a funeral mass for my sister's long-time significant other, Albert Rodd. Al was a firefighter, a wonderful individual whom everyone liked and respected.

As the service progressed, the firefighter's chaplain ascended to the pulpit and recited the firefighter's prayer. As he began his eulogy, he would start with, "I am not just a firefighter," and it struck me that if this is what a firefighter is, then what is a teacher?

The inspiration to write this text is rooted in the belief that we can be what we want to be in the face of enormous odds, and we can derive meaning, strength, and character from the worst situations and translate that into successes.

Oops, let me thank those teachers and others who told me I could not do anything; you were wrong, but you gave me the drive and desire to excel.

For my younger and better teaching professionals, remember; always remember that the *person* sitting in front of you was you when you were a high school student. Treat them with dignity, inspire them, teach them up, and demand—do not ask—they will become better students, better sons or daughters and respectful of values. Demand that they respect their parents and do something for their community.

This work was done for people who need quotes for speeches in education and classroom teachers who would like to teach values through the stories are contained in these pages.

My thoughts are for my mother and father who sacrificed much so I could have a better life than they did. Love never dies; it lives in the heart.

You are not just a teacher because you change lives.

I am not just a teacher. Much is required of you, and much is expected.

I am not just a teacher. "Without continual growth and progress, such words as *improvement, achievement,* and *success* have no meaning." —Benjamin Franklin

I am not just a teacher. "Teachers open the door, you enter by yourself." —A Chinese proverb.

I am not just a teacher. Believe in and achieve greatness in our profession.

I am not just a teacher. One hundred and eighty days of difference, not indifference.

I am not just a teacher. "Be the change you wish to see in the world." —Gandhi.

I am not just a teacher. "Every child is an artist. The problem is how to remain an artist once he grows up." —Pablo Picasso

I am not a teacher. As things change in your life, do not shut out the world. Embrace it and move on to the next level of success.

I am not just a teacher. Even Einstein asked questions.

I am not just a teacher. The choices we make reveal our true character.

I am not just a teacher. Do not get caught, get better.

I am not just a teacher. "This is no time for apathy or complacency. This is a time for vigorous and positive action." —Martin Luther King

I am not just a teacher. The realm of possible resides inside you.

I am not just a teacher. "You have nothing to fear except fear itself." —FDR

I am not just a teacher. You must allow yourself to be great.

I am not just a teacher. Fragility brings out the best of a person.

I am not just a teacher. It would be amazing if we could stop a few minutes and see only what is beautiful.

I am not just a teacher. Kids will learn much more than I will ever know.

I am not just a teacher. This is not here.

I am not just a teacher. True love will hurt when your love passes.

I am not just a teacher. "The only way tomorrow's problems can be solved today is by getting today's population ready to face them." —Arthur F. Corey

I am not just a teacher. When you look at life through the window of your eyes, what do you see that is possible? Do you see anything that is impossible in your classroom?

I am not just a teacher. To be a teacher, you must be the person you want to be.

I am not just a teacher. "It is a wise father who knows his own daughter." —Shakespeare

I am not just a teacher. "In life, unlike chess, life goes on after checkmate." —Isaac Asimov

I am not just a teacher. Teachers who love teaching teach children to love learning.

I am not just a teacher. "Do what you do so well that they will want to see it again and bring their friends." —Walt Disney

I am not just a teacher. "Success is walking from failure to failure with no loss of confidence." —Winston Churchill

I am not just a teacher. In the final analysis, talent can only take you so far, for it is that which is a person's inner strength, desire, and determination that makes person great.

I am not just a teacher. "No great artist ever sees things as they really are. If he did, he would cease to be an artist." —Oscar Wilde

I am not just a teacher. The tapestry of history has no point at which you can cut it and leave the design intelligible.

I am not just a teacher. "You don't do things once in a while. You do all the same way." —Vince Lombardi

I am not just a teacher. Tough ain't enough.

I am not just a teacher. Insanity is doing the same thing the same way and expecting a different outcome.

I am not just a teacher. Raise your child in the realm of what is possible.

I am not just a teacher. A father makes all the difference in his son's life.

I am not just a teacher. Sometimes you do not realize how old you are until you look at your family and friends. There is a gentle easiness tempered by the realization that your life, as you know it, is drawing to its conclusion.

I am not just a teacher. You cannot pay a teacher to teach, but you can't pay a teacher to care. —Maura Collins.

I am not just a teacher. An elementary teacher sent this home to each parent on the first day of school, "If you promise not to believe everything your child says happens in school, I will promise not to believe everything your child says happens at home."

I am not just a teacher. I didn't say it was your fault. I said I wasn't going to blame you!

I am not just a teacher. "Countless words count less than the silent balance between Ying and Yang." —Lao Tzu

I am not just a teacher. "Not until we are lost do we begin to understand ourselves." —Henry David Thoreau

I am not just a teacher. Live your dreams because eternity is a long time. And I, for one, do not want to miss anything.

I am not just a teacher. "Quiet the mind, and the soul will speak." —Bhagvate on "karma"

I am not just a teacher. "I have never understood why it is 'greed' to want to keep the money you've earned, but not greed to want to take somebody else's money." —Thomas Sowell.

I am not just a teacher. "Fathom the hypocrisy of a government that requires every citizen to prove they are insured, but not everyone must prove they are a citizen. Ah, and now, any of those who refuse— or are unable to prove they are citizens—will receive free insurance paid for by those who are forced to buy insurance because they are citizens." —Ben Stein

I am not just a teacher. Teach your content material, but also teach family to your students. And do not be afraid to tell them to thank their parents on holidays and give them the biggest hug and kiss. You can always teach content, but humanity is more important.

I am not just a teacher. Teach them to cope with their fears and aspirations as a surrogate parent, and then tell them about your fears and aspirations as a parent. If you cannot open up, how do expect your students to accept what you say?

I am not just a teacher. Women's rights are human rights.

I am not just a teacher. The farther you look behind, the farther ahead you can look.

I am not just a teacher. Help students find the confidence in their ideas to shape the future.

I am not just a teacher. "If you have always believed that everyone should play by the same rules, and be judged by the same standards, that would have gotten you labeled a radical sixty years ago, a liberal thirty years ago, and a racist today." —Thomas Sowell

I am not just a teacher. I've learned that people will forget what you said, people will forget what you did, but people will never forget how you made them feel.

I am not just a teacher. You can never be just average in a classroom because average will never do in education.

I am not just a teacher. It is what you do as a teacher that defines you.

I am not just a teacher. Passion for teaching is anger and love put together.

I am not just a teacher. If you think education is expensive, try ignorance.

I am not just a teacher. Think for yourself, work together, and share with the world.

I am not just a teacher. A friend knows how you take your coffee, but a great friend adds booze.

I am not just a teacher. Hey, parents, why can't we have a "send your kids to work" while we lie around watching TV all day?

I am not just a teacher. "All you need is ignorance and confidence; then success is sure." —Mark Twain

I am not just a teacher. "A room without books is like a body without a soul." —Cicero

I am not just a teacher. Nations, like men, have their own destiny.

I am not just a teacher. Friends are made by the heart, not by the color of their skin.

I am not just a teacher. Strength always comes from within—teach it, explain it, and live it!

I am not just a teacher. "It has been my experience that folks who have no vices have very few virtues." —Abraham Lincoln

I am not just a teacher. Of all the dignities of the mind, I find goodness and compassion are the greatest.

I am not just a teacher. I believe, like the military, we do this for future generations and those who need a kick to get them going.

I am not just a teacher. A dad is a son's first hero, and a daughter's first love.

I am not just a teacher. People who have never been parents do not have clue when talking about how to educate them and how to discipline them.

I am not just a teacher. "In teaching, you cannot see the fruit of a day's work. It is invisible, and remains so, maybe for twenty years." —Barzun

I am not just a teacher. The easy part is becoming a teacher; the hard part is what makes it great.

I am not just a teacher. Mr. Obama, thanks for all of your hollow promises, but thank you for trickle up poverty. It is really great for families and, of course, low-paid teaching professionals throughout this country.

I am not just a teacher. In order to manipulate the fears of others, you must first master your own.

I am not just a teacher. No child should have to look into the face of death.

I am not just a teacher. "The young man knows the rules. But the old man knows the exceptions." —Unknown.

I am not just a teacher. Do not wait for your ship to come in. Swim out to it.

I am not just a teacher. The harder you try, the more mysterious life becomes.

I am not just a teacher. As time goes by in your career, cherish each moment, embrace the wonderfulness of each day, and love your students like your own.

I am not just a teacher. Life is the sum of the choices we make.

I am not just a teacher. "All men make mistakes, but only wise men learn from their mistakes." —Winston Churchill.

I am not just a teacher. The heart is where your lifelong memories will remain.

I am not just a teacher. Do not look back, you are not going that way.

I am not just a teacher. Just what is it are you seeking as a teacher?

I am not just a teacher. An event in our lives is the day in which we have encountered a mind that startled us.

I am not just a teacher. "You cannot scare me, I'm a teacher." —Unknown

I am not just a teacher. "Treat people as if they were what they ought to be, and you help them become what they're capable of becoming." —Goethe

I am not just a teacher. The true spirit of Christmas lies in your heart.

I am not just a teacher. There is no greater gift than that of friendship.

I am not just a teacher. Your learning is never complete.

I am not just a teacher. It is who we travel through life with that makes a difference

I am not just a teacher. Smile a lot and see how people react to you.

I am not just a teacher. Loyalty and honor beyond anything else.

I am not just a teacher. Decide what you want and then begin by removing the obstacles.

I am not just a teacher. Life is not waiting for the storms to pass; rather, it is learning how to dance in the rain.

I am not just a teacher. Some people search a lifetime for love. When you find it, do not let it go.

I am not just a teacher. But does not anger outweigh guilt?

I am not just a teacher. I am the master of my fate; I am the captain of my ship.

I am not just a teacher. Life is full of possibilities.

I am not just a teacher. The cruelest blow when you are separated is indicating that you are still married. However, nobody asks how long.

I am not just a teacher. Your father reached out and helped you when you were young, as your dad ages gently, or not so gently, now is the time for you to reach out and help him.

I am not just a teacher. Why can't we put our petty differences aside and get on with improving mankind for generations to come?

I am not just a teacher. Anyone who thinks he can be happy and prosperous by letting the government take care of him better take a closer look at the American Indian.

I am not just a teacher. Fear is just a state of mind.

I am not just a teacher. You must be more than a teacher.

I am not just a teacher. "Do one thing every day that scares you." —Eleanor Roosevelt.

I am not just a teacher. "The person who does not read good books has no advantages over the person who cannot read." —Mark Twain

I am not just a teacher. "To thine own self be true." —William Shakespeare

I am not just a teacher; care about what you do with your future.

I am not just a teacher; a man must stand for something or fall for anything.

I am not just a teacher. Listen carefully, President Obama, to Thomas Jefferson, "To take from one because it is thought that his own industry and that of his father's has acquired too much—in order to spare to others, who, or whose fathers, have not exercised equal industry and skill—is to violate arbitrarily the first principle of association, the guarantee to every one of a free exercise of his industry and the fruits acquired by it."

I am not just a teacher. I do not do the same thing each day, nor do I have the same problems each day because every day is extraordinary. I am a good teacher. *Great* sounds too self-serving.

I am not just a teacher. Never regret your calling of being a teacher.

I am not just a teacher. Why do Italians hate Jehovah's Witnesses? Italians hate all witnesses!

I am not just a teacher. "If you make mistakes, there is always another chance for you. You may have a fresh start any moment you choose, for this we call 'failure' is not the falling down but the staying down." —Mary Pickford.

I am not just a teacher. Think of an idea that would change the world, and put it into action.

I am not just a teacher. Older American teacher still in great working condition. No rust, no replacement parts, comfortable interior, and a roomy trunk.

I am not just a teacher. Communication is the most important aspect in a marriage. Without it, there are two ships sailing in different directions.

I am not just a teacher. Knowledge is power.

I am not just a teacher. Do not go around saying the world owes me a living. "The world owes you nothing; it was here first." —Mark Twain.

I am not just a teacher. "I fear nothing, I hope for nothing, and I am free." —Katzanzakis

I am not just a teacher. "Only the educated are free." —Epictetus

I am not just a teacher. Failure is not an option.

I am not just a teacher. Of all the forces that make for a better world, none is as powerful as hope. With hope, one can think, one can work, one can dream. If you have hope, you have everything.

I am not just a teacher. Dear God, I pray for a cure for cancer.

I am not just a teacher. "Some people never go crazy. What truly horrible lives they must lead." —Charles Bukowski

I am not just a teacher. To those who think revenge is justice, you do not have a clue.

I am not just a teacher. Open the shade and let the light in for the energetic, bright, and diverse students who are seated in front of you.

I am not just a teacher. When opportunity and learning collide, the spirit of learning is kindred in the souls of each student seated in front of you.

I am not just a teacher. I do not understand how some people have never been married and experienced the joy, the despair, and the absolute exhilaration of being a parent.

I am not just a teacher. I mold minds.

I am not just a teacher. "But if clothes make the man, naked people have little or no influence on society." —Mark Twain.

I am not just a teacher. Willpower overcomes the odds.

I am not just a teacher. Never judge a book by its movie.

I am not just a teacher. A church is where the humble go to pray.

I am not just a teacher. Never tarnish your parents' memory of you.

I am not just a teacher. Believe and achieve greatness through hard work, understanding your students, and giving them work they will devour.

I am not just a teacher. But when is it that you are considered a man or a woman?

I am not just a teacher. It is not the years in your life that counts; rather it is the life in your years.

I am not just a teacher. But sometimes I feel like a beaver in a land of Formica.

I am not just a teacher. Many will touch your hand, but few will touch your heart, and only one will touch your soul.

I am not just a teacher. "Of all the forces that shape a better world, none is as powerful as hope. With hope, one can think, one can work, one can dream. If you have hope, you have everything." — Sloan-Kettering Cancer Center

I am not just a teacher. But what is the edge of darkness for a teacher? For a student? For our educational system in general?

I am not just a teacher. Life is laughter and compassion.

I am not just a teacher. Listen to Thomas Jefferson again, "I think myself we have more machinery of government than is necessary, too many parasites living on the labor of the industrious."

I am not just a teacher. But when will politicians be held accountable when they screw up and damage an economy that directly impacts on families, jobs, homes, and marriages?

I am not just a teacher. Politicians only answer the questions they want because it puts them in a good light. Heaven forbid if we ever got an honest answer.

I am not just a teacher. The kingdom of God is inside you—use it!

I am not just a teacher. Consciousness is that annoying state between naps.

I am not just a teacher. No child should ever walk alone, and no child should be left behind because of race, color, or national origin.

I am not just a teacher. "There's not an American in this country free until every one of us is free." —Jack Roosevelt Robinson.

I am not just a teacher. But to forget is to repeat.

I am not just a teacher. The more important thing is not to stop questioning. Curiosity has its own reason for existing. One cannot help but be in awe when he contemplates the mysteries of eternity, of life, of the marvelous structure of reality. It is enough if one tries merely to comprehend a little of this mystery every day. Never lose your hold on curiosity. —Albert Einstein

I am not just a teacher. Is compassion a weakness?

I am not just a teacher. Is it what you do in your lifetime that defines you?

I am not just a teacher. We are the guardians of the gate, the new centurions.

I am not just a teacher. Twenty years from now, will you be disappointed by the things you did not do than by the ones you did?

I am not just a teacher. My two sons are my wife's and my contribution to society in the hopes they can fix what we could not.

I am not just a teacher. Are we, as teachers, led by the children?

I am not just a teacher. "Genius is 1 percent inspiration and 99 percent perspiration." —Thomas Edison

I am not just a teacher. "The pen is mightier than the sword." —Edward Butler-Lynton Richelieu

I am not just a teacher. Do not criticize what you cannot understand.

I am not just a teacher. Have you ever had twenty seconds of insane courage?

I am not just a teacher. A child should not have to cry themselves to sleep.

I am not just a teacher. True love never dies because it is in the heart and minds of lovers and loved ones.

I am not just a teacher. The only limitations you have are those you place on yourself.

I am not just a teacher. "What you learn from your yesterdays creates who you are today and directs your path for tomorrow." —Anonymous

I am not just a teacher. How would the classroom change if we offered to our enemies the same suspension of disbelief we extend to our friends?

I am not just a teacher. By not attending a particular class meeting, you do not gain amnesty from the information it encompasses.

I am not just a teacher. But the smallest things make the biggest difference to our lives.

I am not just a teacher. Life and love are cut from the colorful fabric of contradiction and wonder.

I am not just a teacher. "Most things that were once believed impossible are now commonplace." —Unknown

I am not just a teacher. But "vision without action is a dream. Action without vision is aimless. Vision with action will achieve." —Unknown

I am not just a teacher. Thank god for the Shriner's burn hospitals and not only for the job they do with the individual but also for the family. In these cases, the family is an integral part of the individual.

I am not just a teacher. Hold your dreams close to your heart and guard them zealously.

I am not just a teacher. Remember when motorcycles were dangerous and sex was safe?

I am not just a teacher. You should always feel you are special because you are.

I am not just a teacher. If you could make a dream a reality, what would it be?

I am not just a teacher. Friendship is not about whom you have known the longest; it is about those who came and never left your side.

I am not just a teacher. Put your money somewhere else and come to work just like everyone else!

I am not just a teacher. Do not quit, do not give in, do not sell your beliefs and values down the road like a cheap pair of shoes—because sometimes, they are all you have.

I am not just a teacher. Think, connect, and interact with your students.

I am not just a teacher. Is cheating, stealing, or a criminal act worth your name and reputation?

I am not just a teacher. Why bother being good when you can be a *great* teacher?

I am not just a teacher. Why can't we have a decent standard of living?

I am not just a teacher. People fear what they don't understand.

I am not just a teacher. If you can hear the ground trembling, be placed on notice that it is the next generation of humanity that is coming to take their place in the world.

I am not just a teacher. The prayers of my heart are the ones I listen to.

I am not just a teacher. Each day is a gift, why not share it with someone?

I am not just a teacher. There is a dignity in death. And to those like the Elks organization of America who honor their fallen members' memory every year on the first Sunday of December, thank you.

I am not just a teacher. "The hardest part of raising children is teaching them to ride a bicycle. A shaky child on a bicycle for the first time needs both support and freedom. The realization that this is what the child will always need can hit hard." —Sloan Wilson

I am not just a teacher. But if god exists, what would he say to you? What would you say to him? For me, it would be ten more minutes with my father and mother.

I am not just a teacher. But at my age, flowers scare me.

I am not just a teacher. Sunshine has always been on my shoulder. I just never stopped long enough to figure it out.

I am not just a teacher. But if character is destiny, why it is that mankind cannot avoid conflicts?

I am not just a teacher. But when you look into the eyes of the poor, what are you thinking about?

I am not just a teacher. Love people for who they are, be yourself, and go with your gut.

I am not just a teacher. Be curious.

I am not just a teacher. "Attention is the last refuge of failure." —Oscar Wilde

I am not just a teacher. But I believe you get what you give in a classroom.

I am not just a teacher. But I have a wish that each of us could be a hero for one day in our lives because greatness stays with you for the rest of your life.

I am not just a teacher. But you know that kid in the last seat in the last row? If his name begins with a *W*, he has always been seated there and has only had use of black and broken crayons. Why not move him to the front of a row and see what happens? I know I would like a change of scenery if my name began with a *W*!

I am not just a teacher. But I sincerely enjoyed Dick, Jane, and Spot.

I am not just a teacher. But I sometimes feel like the little engine that could when I am teaching at my highest level, and that is about 360 out of 365 days. Like my fellow teachers, we all have bad days we quickly forget. Thank God!

I am not just a teacher. Never accept, "I can handle it from a student." Go the extra mile for that student in acknowledging a problem that he/she thinks they can handle. If we cannot help by listening, then we must direct them to someone who can.

I am not just a teacher. But I think an animal can teach a young person very much about life and death.

I am not just a teacher. The most important knowledge in education is not a master's or doctorate degree, but how to present the class material as if you are sitting in the student work area, listening.

I am not just a teacher. But remember, you young guns, you will be fifty someday and considered old and deadweight by some.

I am not just a teacher. Never wish to be someone else but who you are—that is enough.

I am not just a teacher. Spend time with your children when they are young, for that is when their personality, learning ability, desire to be wanted and valued are most important in their lives.

I am not just a teacher. You may be only one person in the world, but you may also be the world to one student.

I am not just a teacher. I am so old that whenever I eat out, they ask me for money up front.

I am not just a teacher. I believe that a family provides the tranquility every individual must have amidst the dysfunction that is society. It further provides each member a sense of belongingness and calmness that can never be replicated by the hucksters and naysayers who prey on a person's soul.

I am not just a teacher. But only true friends will leave footprints in your heart.

I am not just a teacher. Go observe the gifted teachers in different departments so that you may take what you want from each and craft your teaching style. It is okay to indicate that you want to be better as a young teacher.

I am not just a teacher. To handle others, use your heart and think family.

I am not just a teacher. I would rather live my life as if there is a God, and die to find out there is not, than live my life as if there isn't, and die to find out there is.

I am not just a teacher. What has happened to potential in educators?

I am not just a teacher. Don't slam the door shut. Rather, always leave an opening for when you take emotion out of decisions.

I am not just a teacher. A consultant is a man who knows 101 ways to love a woman but does not love one.

I am not just a teacher. But we all stand up for children every single day of our lives.

I am not just a teacher. If there is a better solution, find it!

I am not just a teacher; the sum of us is greater than all our parts.

I am not just a teacher. To handle yourself, use your head.

I am not just a teacher. Do you like yourself?

I am not just a teacher. Be bright, be creative, but most importantly, be compassionate.

I am not just a teacher. Nobody takes anything away from you. Nobody gives their dignity up for it is inside you and me.

I am not just a teacher. Anger is only one letter short of danger.

I am not just a teacher. I'm so old all of my friends in heaven will think I didn't make it!

I am not just a teacher. Great minds discuss ideas; average minds discuss events; small minds discuss people.

I am not just a teacher. If someone betrays you once, it is his fault; if he betrays you twice, it is your fault.

I am not just a teacher. I have learned that life is like a roll of toilet paper. The closer it gets to the end, the faster it goes.

I am not just a teacher. He who loses a friend loses much more.

I am not just a teacher. He who loses faith loses all.

I am not just a teacher. Does there ever come a time when being something or someone justifies trampling on people, tradition, or position in one's lifetime?

I am not just a teacher. You can only be who you are, know your strengths, and improve your weaknesses.

I am not just a teacher. But birthdays are good for you because the more you have, the longer you live.

I am not just a teacher. One good thing about Alzheimer's is that you get to meet new people every day.

I am not just a teacher. Learn from the mistakes of others. You cannot live long enough to make them all yourself.

I am not just a teacher. Death is a betrayal to the lives we all live.

I am not just a teacher. When a questioner has boxed in a politician

I am not just a teacher. There is no beginning or end for a circle of friends.

I am not just a teacher. But there is connectivity between teacher and student, man and wife, father/mother and children that creates a bond for life that never dies. The images, the stories seem to bring about fond memories of days gone by that are still fresh and vibrant in people's minds. Today is yesterday once again.

I am not just a teacher. Please support bingo and keep grand-mothers off the streets.

I am not just a teacher. But as long as you hold someone in your heart, you will never lose them. *Never*!

I am not just a teacher. We all possess the gift of teaching, but what we need to remember is that a gift is only as good as how much hard work you put into it.

I am not just a teacher. "From what we get, we can make a living; what we give, however, makes a life." —Arthur Ashe

I am not just a teacher. We light the fires that will burn brightly for eternity.

I am not just a teacher. I am hopeful and endlessly surprised at how surprised I can be.

I am not just a teacher. Trust your hunches. They are usually based on facts filed away just below the conscious level.

I am not just a teacher. I have learned that money does not buy you class.

I am not just a teacher. Never judge a young adult by his clothes, the length of his hair, or you will be judged also.

I am not just a teacher. The time is always right to do what is right.

I am not just a teacher. "Logic will get you from A to B. Imagination will take to everywhere." —Albert Einstein

I am not just a teacher. But when did my wild oats turn into prunes and bran?

I am not just a teacher. Never mistake knowledge for wisdom. One helps you make a living, and the other helps you make a life.

I am not just a teacher. The highest reward for a person's toil is not what they get for it, but rather what they become by it.

I am not just a teacher. Truth has no special time.

I am not just a teacher. Love, adventure, character, intelligence, emotional maturity, and friendship should always be part of your teaching soul.

I am not just a teacher. "Always read stuff that will make you look good if you die in the middle of it."—P. J. O'Rourke

I am not just a teacher. "The greatest mistake you can make in life is to be continually fearing you will make one". —E. Hubbard

I am not just a teacher. "Learning is not attained by chance; it must be sought for with an ardor and attended to with diligence." —Abigail Adams

I am not just a teacher. Make your classroom a place where students come to learn. Make that classroom have sensory appeal and reinforce your class as a safe room where students are valued.

I am not just a teacher. Faith believes something is true in the absence of facts.

I am not just a teacher. "When I was a boy of fourteen, my father was so ignorant I could hardly stand to have the old man around. But when I got to be twenty-one, I was astounded at how much the old man had learned in seven years." —Mark Twain

I am not just a teacher. Lives are not perfect circles, nor are my young adults.

I am not just a teacher. You need to enjoy life.

I am not just a teacher. Greatness in education can and must be passed on!

I am not just a teacher. Do not be a phony. Kids will figure you out for what you are and reject you. Be yourself, for nobody understands you like you.

I am not just a teacher. What if?

I am not just a teacher. Live for the moment; life is too short.

I am not just a teacher. Dreams are who we are and what we become, so prepare your dreams for success.

I am not just a teacher. The strength and depth of a teacher's comportment is what sets him/her apart from others in the world. They can tell presidents, parents, and students what is right with one look. Students recognize inner strength for what it is: *caring*.

I am not just a teacher. I have learned that we should be glad God does not give us everything we pray for.

I am not just a teacher. In the final analysis, talent alone takes you only so far; for it is that inner strength, drive, and determination that makes a person great!

I am not just a teacher. What would you do if you found a message in a bottle?

I am not just a teacher. Look at your lesson plans through the portal of your eyes and ask yourself, "Is this the best plan today, and how can I make it better, more interesting, more challenging?

I am not just a teacher. "An archeologist is the best husband any woman can have. The older she gets, the more interested he is in her." —Agatha Christie

I am not just a teacher. I am also a football official, and when I stand on that gridiron prior to a game standing at attention and listening to the national anthem, I sometimes look through the far goalposts to see the flag whirling in the breeze. The emotions that swirl through my mind of freedom, being an American, family, and friends no longer alive are truly dramatic.

I am not just a teacher. If you say something inappropriate, have the courage to apologize for it. Your stature will grow in the student's view.

I am not just a teacher. We live in darkness until we can see ourselves.

I am not just a teacher. "Insist on yourself, never imitate." —Ralph Waldo Emerson

I am not just a teacher. I am experiencing the midsummer of my life.

I am not just a teacher. Cherish people with talent, regardless of their age.

I am not just a teacher. "You live only once, but if you do it right, once is enough." —Mae West

I am not just a teacher. But isn't every day above ground a good day?

I am not just a teacher. But I know that kids growing up hard with ultimately be great workers, husbands, and parents.

I am not just a teacher. We teach family where there is none.

I am not just a teacher. "You know, Willie Wonka said it best, 'We are the makers of dreams, the dreamers of dreams.' We grew up as kids having dreams, but now we are too sophisticated as adults, as a nation, we stopped dreaming. We should always have dreams." —Herb Brooks

I am not just a teacher. What is a person's life worth if there is not an expectation of tomorrow?

I am not just a teacher. Love and inspiration makes people a family.

I am not just a teacher. If I read the obits and do not find my name there, it is cause for a big time celebration.

I am not just a teacher. There is only love for teaching.

I am not just a teacher. Every day is a blank canvas.

I am not just a teacher. "I didn't grow up with my father, but he is the one who mentored me and told me what I needed to do without telling me what to do—that is a tough thing for a father to do." — Colonel Al Aycock

I am only a teacher. Loneliness in decision is part of life.

I am not just a teacher. Turbulence in life is a prerequisite for character.

I am not just a teacher. Those who mind do not matter, and those who matter do.

I am not just a teacher. I'm not losing my hair, rather I am gaining more skin to tan.

I am not just a teacher. Passion is your way of presenting concepts that inspire you. Now reach inside all of your students and grasp their passion and bring it out of them. Your best learning takes place when you remove all the restraints and you search for knowledge in your students' souls.

I am not just a teacher. I have learned that it is those small daily happenings that make life spectacular.

I am not just a teacher. But do we not find out what meddle a person has when they fail every now and then?

I am not just a teacher. Blondes really do not have all the fun, thank God!

I am not just a teacher. Measure your teaching and coaching life in how you taught boys and girls to be men and women ready to take their places in society, then they can measure you.

I am not just a teacher. At the touch of love, everyone becomes a poet.

I am not just a teacher. "It is not flesh and blood but the heart which makes us fathers and sons." —Schiller

I am not just a teacher. Making the best choices possible should be your passion.

I am not just a teacher. Believe in me because I am you.

I am not just a teacher. Size, looks, and age will not dictate talent.

I am not just a teacher. The most important thing to hear is what is not being said.

I am not just a teacher. Every time I can think of one thousand reasons to leave teaching because of this and that, there is but one reason to stay: those students! They are my new children.

I am not just a teacher. But are not acts of kindness inherent in all human beings?

I am not just a teacher. Be constructive, not destructive. You win in one and lose big time in the other.

I am not just a teacher. A real friend walks in when the rest of the world walks out. Thank you, Cookie, Dennis, Annie, Mike, and Mark.

I am not just a teacher. But retirement is twice as much wife, half as much money.

I am not just a teacher. But is there not a oneness with God in our daily lives?

I am not just a teacher. "It's what you learn after you know it all that counts." —John Wooden

I am not just a teacher. Under everyone's hard shell, there is someone who wants to be loved and appreciated.

I am not just a teacher. Worshipping money is the surest way to self-destruction and ruination.

I am not just a teacher. Dance like there is no one watching.

I am not just a teacher. Kind words can be short and easy to speak, but their echoes are truly endless.

I am not just a teacher. But I wish every young boy and girl could sit on a porch with their grandfather or grandmother and have them explain life and history. I am sure it would be a treat.

I am not just a teacher. My wife always gives me sound advice—99 percent sound and 1 percent advice.

I am not just a teacher. The toughest life to save is your own.

I am not just a teacher. Sometimes life is too damn hard and really unfair. What then are your options?

I am not just a teacher. What separates winners from losers in life is that winners keep on getting up on that horse until they no longer fall off.

I am not just a teacher. But we have to choose between yesterday and tomorrow.

I am not just a teacher. "The essential skill of parenting is making up answers. When an experienced father is driving down the road and his son/daughter asks him how much a building weighs, he does not hesitate for a second, 'three thousand four hundred and fifty-seven tons,' he says." —Dave Berry

I am not just a teacher. I honor the past, celebrate the present, and realize the future.

I am not just a teacher. If you obey all the rules, you will miss all the fun.

I am not just a teacher. "Friends…they cherish each other's hopes; they are kind to each other's dreams." —Thoreau

I am not just a teacher. Success requires more backbone than wishbone.

I am not just a teacher. We make a living from what we get, but we make a life from what we give.

I am not just a teacher. To ignore facts does not change the facts.

I am not just a teacher. There is always more than one way to solve any problem. The problem is some think there is only one way—their way.

I am not just a teacher. Friends are like flowers, they never fade.

I am not just a teacher. Never a failure. Rather, I have found many ways that do not work.

I am not just a teacher. Nothing great was ever achieved without enthusiasm.

I am not just a teacher. The less time I have to work, the more I get done.

I am not just a teacher. Show your friends just how much you care.

I am not just a teacher. My sons knew that whenever and wherever they needed me, I would be there!

I am not just a teacher. A student's name is his/hers. Learn how to pronounce and spell it. It does make a difference.

I am not just a teacher. I place my whole heart and soul into teaching and hope I have given enough.

I am not just a teacher. Life and death are temporary, but freedom lives on forever.

I am not just a teacher. When you look long into an abyss, the abyss looks into you.

I am not just a teacher. Embracing the opportunity to be a classroom teacher is the greatest privilege ever accorded an individual.

I am not just a teacher. Leonardo DaVinci invented scissors. Also, it took him ten years to paint the Mona Lisa's lips.

I am not just a teacher. Leonardo DaVinci could write with one hand and draw with the other at the same time.

I am not just a teacher. The name Wendy was made up from the book *Peter Pan,* and prior to that there was never a recorded Wendy before.

I am not just a teacher. "We should not mourn the deaths of these brave soldiers. Rather, we should thank God such men lived." —Gen. George Patton

I am not just a teacher. Leadership is action, not reaction!

I am not just a teacher. Do not teach from fear. Rather, teach from strength and the power to take the first step forward as a new professional.

I am not just a teacher. Give me parents we can work with, and I will show you instilled values in the student from the home.

I am not just a teacher. I do not always know the key(s) to success, but the key to failure is to try and please everyone.

I am not just a teacher. I like you because of who you are to me—a true friend.

I am not just a teacher. But the world is divided into people who do things and people who get the credit.

I am not just a teacher. Don't you just love it when the state schedules hearings for changes in your retirement benefits but does it so that your voice goes unheard? Ah, Massachusetts democracy. It is like Billy Bulger, Tom Finneran, and Bill Weld were still running the state. Did any of them plug the holes in the big dig?

I am not just a teacher. I can see the sun shining.

I am not just a teacher. I hate teaching to a state-mandated test because it takes away my creativity.

I am not just a teacher. I learn from my students.

I am not just a teacher. The *Guinness Book of World Records* holds the record for being the book most often stolen from libraries.

I am not just a teacher. I hope you learn humility by being humiliated, and that you learn honesty by being cheated on.

I am not just a teacher. To understand a man, you need to know his memories.

I am not just a teacher. Any child can tell you that the sole purpose of a middle name is so he can tell when he is really in trouble.

I am not just a teacher. He that can have patience will have what he wants.

I am not just a teacher Choices are what make us who we are.

I am not just a teacher. Why is it that if you are bright, good-looking, and talented, some people try to run you down?

I am not just a teacher. Hey, you young teachers, listen to the voices of experience because you will be that voice someday.

I am not just a teacher. Judge a person by who they are, not what you want them to be.

I am not just a teacher. The greatest gifts you can give your child are responsibility and the wings of independence.

I am not just a teacher. Manners are a happy way of doing things.

I am not just a teacher. "People acting together as a group can accomplish things which no individual acting alone would ever hope to bring about." —Franklin Delano Roosevelt

I am not just a teacher. Painting is easy when you do not know how, but very difficult when you do.

I am not just a teacher. Correction does much, but encouragement does more.

I am not just a teacher. Never ask if a student in your class is a brother or a sister of a student you had in class. Do it after class and quietly.

I am not just a teacher. When all else fails, read the instructions.

I am not just a teacher. Maybe I am stupid, but how can a state's governor help place private charter schools into his/her state, give them public funds that were meant for public education, and then chastise the public schools for not doing their job? Maybe I am not the stupid one!

I am not just a teacher. A friend will come bail you out of jail, but a *true* friend will be sitting next to you saying, "We screwed up, but we had fun!" I would be proud to be *that* friend.

I am not just a teacher. You must be a blue neck if you would rather vacation on Martha's Vineyard than Six Flags.

I am not just a teacher. I am electric! Take my hand and start the transference of knowledge for the rest of your life.

I am not just a teacher. I gladly accept differences because all students do not learn alike and at the same time, rather they learn when they know they have been accepted for who they are.

I am not just a teacher. But how about state legislatures and governors who want to limit your rights to bargain collectively and unilaterally cut your health benefits? Why do they not go to the sources and ask, "When is enough enough"? Aren't these people supposed to protect the ordinary Joes of the world?

I am not just a teacher. Just as there are no little people or unimportant lives, there is no insignificant work.

I am not just a teacher. Discoveries are often made by not following instructions, by going off the main road, by trying the untried.

I am not just a teacher. Who are people who criticize public education scores? Legislators? Governors? Others? You have told us we cannot do any other job except teach, why don't you swap jobs with me? I know I can do a better job than a governor because he just does not understand anything except running for president and looking good!

I am not just a teacher. But I would sure like to possess the inner strength and determination of a Rosa Parks and give it to those who have lost their direction in life.

I am not just a teacher. I hope for war to end and return young men and women to the safety of the United States.

I am not just a teacher. You might be a blue neck if you do not know anyone with at least two first names (i.e., Joe Bob, Faye Ellen, Billie Bob, and Mary Jo).

I am not just a teacher. I am Christa McAuliffe. I am Darwin. I am John Dewey. I am Owen B. Channing.

I am not just a teacher. "If you do not invest much in yourself, then defeat doesn't hurt very much and winning isn't very exciting." —Dick Vermeil

I am not just a teacher. I hope nobody gives you a new car when you turn sixteen.

I am not just a teacher. Thank you, Mr. Hayes, for telling me I would not amount to anything. You gave me drive, determination, singleness of purpose—and most importantly, goals for life.

I am not just a teacher. "Everything on earth has a purpose— every person a mission." —Mourning Dove (Salish)

I am not just a teacher. It would be good if at least one time you can see puppies born and your old dog put to sleep.

I am not just a teacher. I hope you get a black eye fighting for something you believe in.

I am not just a teacher. Observe an altercation, but try not to get involved because each of the combatants may hate you.

I am not just a teacher. I hope you learn to dig in the dirt and read books.

I am not just a teacher. I want to challenge my students every single day and have them challenge me so we both can be better.

I am not just a teacher. Power is knowledge, and knowledge is power.

I am not just a teacher. I believe in wonderment.

I am not just a teacher. I worry about others and their plights.

I am not just a teacher. I look for personality traits beyond high-stakes testing in my students.

I am not just a teacher. I believe in the heart and soul of a person, not how they walk and talk or the color of their skin.

I am not just a teacher. The difference between the impossible and the possible lies in a person's determination.

I am not just a teacher. Education is learning what you didn't even know you didn't know.

I am not just a teacher. You are not famous until your mother knows about it.

I am not just a teacher. "I was given a tremendous gift in terms of athleticism. Maybe it was because I wasn't so confident in other areas." —Mia Hamm

I am not just a teacher. A young person should be raised by their biological parents to understand love and affection.

I am not just a teacher. I understand that life goes on no matter what.

I am not just a teacher. How long will I live?

I am not just a teacher. But have you not looked at the sky and wondered if we are really alone?

I am not just a teacher. I pretend to be a Major League baseball player because dreams, no matter how old you are, Joe Hardy, are what have made America what it is, the land of opportunity.

I am not just a teacher. I am a pragmatist trapped in a politically correct world.

I am not just a teacher. Would it not be great if we could do something with our lives that changes the face of humanity for a lifetime?

I am not just a teacher. When you learn to use computers, I hope you will also learn to add and subtract in your head.

I am not just a teacher. I hope you get teased by your friends when you have your first crush on a boy/girl, and when you talk back to your mom, that you learn what Ivory soap tastes like.

I am not just a teacher. I don't care if you try beer once, but I hope you don't like it. If a friend offers you dope or a joint, I hope you realize he/she is not your friend.

I am not just a teacher. I hope you make time to sit on a porch or deck with your grandma/grandpa and go fishing with your uncle.

I am not just a teacher. I hope you possess the spirit and wonderment of Christmas for as long as you live.

I am not just a teacher. If I die before you do, I will go to heaven and keep an eye on you while I am waiting for you.

I am not just a teacher. I have heard the words of Dr. King, FDR, Julius Cesar, and Jesus.

I am not just a teacher. Why can we not discuss religion in public schools? Is it not a place where people exchange ideas and learn from others without oppression?

I am not just a teacher. "Aim for the moon, if you miss, you may hit a star." —W. C. Stone

I am not just a teacher. How can you live knowing there is not a closure to someone's life?

I am not just a teacher. I *hate* the saying, "Perception is reality." It is rarely spoken by a truthful person, just a user in my opinion.

I am not just a teacher. I can hear my son's guitar talking.

I am not just a teacher. I explain dignity and self-esteem.

I am not just a teacher. "Receive everything that happens to you in simplicity". —Rash

I am not just a teacher. The sum of all your fears is yourself.

I am not just a teacher. See the pride and joy through the tears of the gold medal winners in the Special Olympics.

I am not just a teacher. I will lift you up when you cannot reach.

I am not just a teacher. I enjoy meeting new people and doing things for the first time.

I am not just a teacher. How do you really deal with a fifteen-year-old who has just lost his dad to a heart attack?

I am not just a teacher. Get used to meeting each blossoming day, a day of new life, where only you make the entry on a blank page.

I am not just a teacher. I will lose my faith in education every now and then, but my refuge is the students I serve, and they will restore my faith in education.

I am not just a teacher. I have one mind, one body, and one direction that always points to success.

I am not just a teacher. I teach direction in the classroom, family, and one's life in addition to course content.

I am not just a teacher. I reject exploitation at any level to any person anywhere in the world.

I am not just a teacher. When I stop encouraging my students to reach for the stars, then I will be too dammed old and should retire.

I am not just a teacher. May you feel sorrow at funerals and joy during the holidays.

I am not just a teacher. I hope your mother punished you when you threw a baseball through your neighbor's window and that she hugs you to death and kisses you at Hanukkah/Christmas time when you give her a plaster mold of your hand.

I am not just a teacher. I love mistakes because it gives me a time to teach, reinforce, and explain that there is usually more right than wrong in a student's solution.

I am not just a teacher. But when you have a really bad day, will you come to doubt all of your beliefs? If so, remember there is always another day and an opportunity to be absolutely terrific!

I am not just a teacher. Treat those students like they are your own, and you will never go too far wrong.

I am not just a teacher. Life is not a true-or-false test or a Scantron sheet, but rather it is a discussion question.

I am not just a teacher. "You can never meet everyone's expectations. It is hard enough to meet your own." —Andrea Jaeger

I am not just a teacher. I speak *to* my students, not *at* them. I want and encourage them to be independent thinkers.

I am not just a teacher. We must decide to do what is best with the time we are given.

I am not just a teacher. "What other people may find in poetry or art museums, I find in the flight of a good drive." —Arnold Palmer.

I am not just a teacher. I wish I had more than just one lifetime to give back what I have received over the years.

I am not just a teacher. If you were running in a race and the person in front of you tripped and fell, would you stop and pick that person up during the race or during life?

I am not just a teacher. I gave to the extent that I lost my marriage.

I am not just a teacher. I am human and possess all the frailties and emotions that everyone has but will not admit to it. Just stubborn, I guess.

I am not just a teacher. Imagine.

I am not just a teacher. We must challenge students to be academically, socially, and emotionally mature human beings.

I am not just a teacher. We are always given a second chance, third chance, and fourth chance. You never know what impact that will have on a student's life.

I am not just a teacher. We teach strength when you are weak.

I am not just a teacher. I offer you my educational hand and teach you how to be an independent thinker.

I am not just a teacher. "Sometimes a player's greatest challenge is coming to grips with his role on the team." —Scottie Pippen

I am not just a teacher. I remember my high school teachers who showed me strength in times of adversity. Thank you, Marion Diemond and Fran O'Brien.

I am not just a teacher. I am a father, a husband, and a citizen of the United States of America.

I am not just a teacher. I remember my mom and dad being as proud of me, as I am of my sons, Michael and Mark, and their accomplishments.

I am not just a teacher. I inspire people to reach for the stars and beyond.

I am not just a teacher. I give and give and give again.

I am not just a teacher. I challenge the student's soul

I am not just a teacher. I explain and demonstrate what courage is and then inspire my students to be courageous by standing up for their beliefs.

I am not just a teacher. I do not see color.

I am not just a teacher. Why will people assume a fifteen-year-old can always make the correct decision if they have never been shown how to in the home.

I am not just a teacher. I am a role model for adult behavior.

I am not just a teacher. I am a surrogate parent with the entire responsibilities attendant to that trust.

I am not just a teacher. I am a doctor, a psychologist, and a disciplinarian.

I am not just a teacher. I am compassionate when I encounter an abused student and equally outraged that this could happen to one of my students.

I am not just a teacher. I teach brotherhood.

I am not just a teacher. I am your eyes when you cannot see.

I am not just a teacher. Why do croutons come in an airtight package? Aren't they just stale bread to begin with?

I am not just a teacher. Are you ever wrong and admit it?

I am not just a teacher. What's wrong with reading *The Little Train that Could* to your high school students? Does this book not show us prejudice, standing up and saying, "I think I can, I think I can, and yes, I can."

I am not just a teacher. I must elevate the learning level of each and every student in my classroom because they will need that education to compete in the global market.

I am not just a teacher. I teach dignity and respect for each and every man, woman, and child on God's earth.

I am not just a teacher. But if lawyers are disbarred and clergymen defrocked, does it follow that electricians can be delighted, musicians denoted, cowboys deranged, models deposed, tree surgeons debarked, and dry cleaners depressed?

I am not just a teacher. I have patience beyond those of mortal men and women, but I cannot leap off tall buildings, but I will continue to practice.

I am not just a teacher. I show how attitude reflects leadership.

I am not just a teacher. I teach teamwork, unity, and strength.

I am not just a teacher. I see real sickness and suffering on the inside but outwardly encourage and support that young man or woman during their hour of need and comfort.

I am not just a teacher. I must work well with my fellow professionals in order to insure a smooth educational experience for all.

I am not just a teacher. I absorb all the politicians' degrading remarks about the teaching profession and move on in spite of it because they really do not know how to teach. And usually, if given the chance, they will mess up a young person's education by allowing taxpayers' dollars to be used for private or charter schools.

I am not just a teacher. I do not accept *can't*.

I am not just a teacher. Keep on telling young people it is okay to do something when you know it is wrong. Tell them it is all right to steal, to do drugs with their parents—but never tell them that there are consequences.

I am not just a teacher. I will not accept bullying.

I am not just a teacher. I will not have any patience with orders without a sound educational foundation.

I am not just a teacher. I will demand quality from my students, and anything less is unacceptable.

I am not just a teacher. "When you reach for the top, keep on climbing." —Proverb

I am not just a teacher. I believe that when you move beyond your dreams and achieve success, you have finally become free.

I am not just a teacher. I have grown to understand that people who have AIDS are really human beings who are special and deserve our respect.

I am not just a teacher. But I am one who is just amazed whenever a plane flies with me in it.

I am not just a teacher. I recognize that a person's religion is personal and unique.

I am not just a teacher. Will the judges please enforce the laws as they stand even if they do not agree with them? You know that is why you were made a judge.

I am not just a teacher. I am involved in my school because I have a responsibility to see the student beyond the classroom.

I am not just a teacher. I try inspiring students too. As Robert Kennedy once said, "Some people see things that are and ask why. I dream things that never were and ask why not."

I am not just a teacher. I am an observer of human behavior.

I am not just a teacher. I am an advocate for my students.

I am not just a teacher. I am a lifelong learner.

I am not just a teacher. I think the movie character ET would threaten people.

I am not just a teacher. We do not know how well we have done our job with our students for ten years.

I am not just a teacher. We give and expect respect from the students and the individuals we effectively deal with every day of our lives.

I am not just a teacher. I worry about my sons and wife every day I am alive, even though love transcends the bounds of time and distance.

I am not just a teacher. My age has nothing to do with my classroom effectiveness.

I am not just a teacher. I am a leader, a role model, and an activist in my community for all things that benefit young adults.

I am not just a teacher. I refuse to acquiesce to supporting ideas and dogmas that are contrary to my own principles.

I am not just a teacher. I encourage and support students to help their communities in constructive ways, not because it looks good, but because they are giving back to a community that has given to them.

I am not just a teacher. I encourage students to become doctors, accountants, nurses, salesmen, and labor workers because in each and every student, there is a burning desire to do something or be someone that drives individuals to be the best. The trick is making sure the student understands that when preparation meets opportunity, success should follow.

I am not just a teacher. I look into the eyes of poverty and ask why the richest nation in the world cannot support its weak, its poor, and its destitute. Then I look at the congress and the president for answers that I never get.

I am not just a teacher. Education's purpose is to replace an empty mind with an open one.

I am not just a teacher. We often have two lives. The one we learn with, and the one we live with.

I am not just a teacher. A great teacher never strives to explain his vision, he simply invites you to stand beside him and see for yourself.

I am not just a teacher. Children are likely to live up to what you believe of them.

I am not just a teacher. You are only as good as your next teaching point.

I am not just a teacher. Treat a young adult as though he already is the person he is capable of becoming.

I am not just a teacher. Ask the student what we can do together to make her/him a better student today.

I am not just a teacher. Encourage your students to think like the little engine that could.

I am not just a teacher. We must inspire children and young adults.

I am not just a teacher. The trick is growing up without growing old.

I am not just a teacher. The future is not what it used to be.

I am not just a teacher. A life is not significant except for its impact on other lives.

I am not just a teacher. But a man/woman has to have goals for a day and a lifetime.

I am not just a teacher. Every day is a new opportunity. You can build on yesterday's successes or put its failures behind and start over again. That is the way life is, and that is how education must be.

I am not just a teacher. You owe it to yourself to be the best you can be in the classroom.

I am not just a teacher. Without hope, there is nothing.

I am not just a teacher. Do not try to be somebody you are not.

I am not just a teacher. Be a communicator not a silent movie.

I am not just a teacher. Take the time to thank the people who helped you along the way.

I am not just a teacher. Never be ashamed to hug and kiss your dad or mom in public.

I am not just a teacher. Life is to be savored, not gulped.

I am not just a teacher. There is more to life than money and power. Live it!

I am not just a teacher. Teaching allows us to stay young at heart.

I am not just a teacher. You cannot beat the person who never gives up.

I am not just a teacher. More men fail through lack of purpose than lack of talent.

I am not just a teacher. Success is being truly happy at what you do.

I am not just a teacher. Enthusiasm has to be generated day in and day out. It is the only way to teach for learning permanence.

I am not just a teacher. Hugs are for sharing.

I am not just a teacher. Fight hate and promote tolerance.

I am not just a teacher. What we anticipate seldom happens, but what we least expect generally happens.

I am not just a teacher. Education is the fundamental method of social progress and reform.

I am not just a teacher. When you see death for the first time, understand it is nature's way—but more importantly, celebrate that person's life.

I am not just a teacher. Be genuine to your students, they can figure out a phony in five seconds.

I am not just a teacher. Imagine peace!

I am not just a teacher. I am a mom, a dad, friend, coach, counselor, actor, comedian for my students—and it is an honor.

I am not just a teacher. Nations, like men, have their own destiny.

I am not just a teacher. But winning may not always be winning. Losing is not always losing if respect is the final outcome.

I am not just a teacher. But aren't values simply the beliefs that guide your life and set you apart from others?

I am not just a teacher. Did you know that those who spend their time protecting others are usually the ones that really need someone to protect them?

I am not just a teacher. The three most difficult things to say are "I love you," "sorry," and "help me."

I am not just a teacher. A year from now, you may wish you had started today.

I am not just a teacher. But did you know that it is easier to say what you feel in writing than saying it to someone face-to-face? But did you know that it has more value when you say it to their face?

I am not just a teacher. A billion minutes ago, Jesus was alive.

I am not just a teacher. A billion hours ago, our ancestors were living in the Stone Age.

I am not just a teacher. Your will turns thoughts into reality.

I am not just a teacher. A billion days ago. No one walked on the earth on two feet.

I am not just a teacher. When something is new and improved, which is it? If it's new, then there has never been anything before it. If it's an improvement, then there must have been something before it, and it couldn't be new.

I am not just a teacher. When people say, "It is always the last place you look." Duh, of course it is. Why the hell would you keep on looking after you have found it?

I am not just a teacher. The X factor in being a professional educator is talent.

I am not just a teacher. I'm standing in my heart.

I am not just a teacher. You first get the inkling that you are old at twenty-six when someone addresses you as sir or ma'am.

I am not just a teacher. You have to leave the past behind you before you can go forward.

I am not just a teacher. Television is called a medium. It is called that because nothing is well done.

I am not just a teacher. What is on your mind? If you will allow me the understatement.

I am not just a teacher. But how does the tin man go to the bathroom without rusting?

I am not just a teacher. Hanging is too good for a man who makes puns. He should be drawn and quoted.

I am not just a teacher. A committee is a group of men who individually can do nothing but, as a group, decides that nothing can be done. (Ah, the political system at its best.)

I am not just a teacher. It is always difficult to do the simple things in life.

I am not just a teacher. But what is better than when one person who has been through a serious illness and survived and then reaches out to another such individual and imparts reassurance?

I am not just a teacher. I have just returned from Boston. It is the only sane thing to do if you find yourself there.

I am not just a teacher. There are worse things in life besides death. Have you ever spent an evening with an insurance salesman?

I am not just a teacher. I don't want to achieve immortality through my work. I want to achieve it through not dying.

I am not just a teacher. You can only be young once, but you can always be immature.

I am not just a teacher. Drawing on my fine command of the English language, I said nothing.

I am not just a teacher. Happiness is having good health and a bad memory.

I am not just a teacher. Always keep the memory of your mother and father in your heart.

I am not just a teacher. Life is too short to waste time hating anyone.

I am not just a teacher. When I was a boy, the Dead Sea only had a virus.

I am not just a teacher. Too bad the only people who know how to run the country are driving cabs and cutting hair.

I am not just a teacher. Ending a sentence with a preposition is something up with which I will not put.

I am not just a teacher. Although prepared for martyrdom, I preferred that it be postponed.

I am not just a teacher. "I believe that any man's finest hour is that moment when he worked his heart out in a good cause and lies exhausted on the field of battle." —Vince Lombardi

I am not just a teacher. Early to bed and early to rise probably indicates an unskilled worker.

I am not just a teacher. But if the Jacksonville Jaguars are known as the Jags and the Tampa Bay Buccaneers are known as the Bucks, what does that make the Tennessee Titans?

I am not just a teacher. But the trouble with children is that they are not returnable.

I am not just a teacher. If you can keep your head when everyone around you is losing theirs, you probably just do not understand the situation!

I am not just a teacher. Do not take yourself so seriously; no one else does.

I am not just a teacher. If a pig loses its voice, is it disgruntled?

I am not just a teacher. When your time to retire comes, recognize it and enjoy those small things you used to be too busy to notice.

I am not just a teacher. Horse sense is the thing a horse has which prevents him from betting on people.

I am not just a teacher. Embrace the meaning of Christmas.

I am not just a teacher. In the star shines the hope. In the heart lives the dream… a bright and shining world at peace.

I am not just a teacher. And you are not just a parent.

I am not just a teacher. No truth is ever a lie.

I am not just a teacher. Do you ever wonder about those people who spend $2 for a bottle of Evian water? Spelled backward: *naïve*.

I am not just a teacher. If four out of five people suffer from diarrhea, does that mean that one enjoys it?

I am not just a teacher. Caring is not optional for a teacher!

I am not just a teacher. Bring kids into your world, do not be led into theirs.

I am not just a teacher. Life is not always fair, get over it! It is still good!

I am not just a teacher: You will never be a leader until you have lost something.

I am not just a teacher. There is no finish line.

I am not just a teacher. So who you going to blame for this adversity?

I am not just a teacher. You must be prepared, unselfish, and passionate in order to feel the heartbeat of your class. This would be a good lesson for the so-called leaders of the world.

I am just a teacher. But if you are able to go to church, a mosque, or synagogue without fear of harassment, arrest, torture, or death, you are happier than three billion persons in the world.

I am not just a teacher. If your parents are alive and still married, then you are a rarity.

I am not just a teacher. You do not have to win every argument, agree to disagree.

I am not just a teacher. "I am only one, but I am still one. I cannot do everything, but still I can do something. I will not refuse to do something I can do." —Helen Keller

I am not just a teacher. Presence is the gift of life.

I am not just a teacher. Isn't a woman in love beautiful in your eyes?

I am not just a teacher. Don't get by, get better!

I am not just a teacher. Work like you do not need the money. Love like you have never been hurt. And sing like nobody is listening.

I am not just a teacher. But if you tell the truth, you do not have to remember three lies.

I am not just a teacher. Always find good people and emulate them.

I am not just a teacher. Have you ever hit bottom and wanted to quit? Where did you find the courage to continue on? It is called *character*.

I am not just a teacher. Let us not be stopped by that which divides us, but look for that which unites us.

I am not just a teacher. Love for money is sorrowful for both parties.

I am not just a teacher. "God puts us all in each other's lives to impact one another in some way. Look for God in others. The best and most beautiful things cannot be seen or touched—they must be felt with the heart." —Helen Keller

I am not just a teacher. You want to get angry with your God? Go ahead. He has huge shoulders.

I am not just a teacher. But if any relationship has to be a secret, then it is not worth being in.

I am not just a teacher. Do you really believe in yourself and your life?

I am not just a teacher. "In a completely rational society, the best of us would aspire to be teachers and the rest of us would have to settle for something less because passing civilization along from one generation to the next ought to be the highest honor and the highest responsibility anyone could have." —Lee Iacocca

I am not just a teacher. No one can walk backward into the future.

I am not just a teacher. The world may hurdle on by you, but greatness, in its many forms, will always remain with you.

I am not just a teacher. Life is too short for pity parties. Get busy living or get busy dying.

I am not just a teacher. You can get through anything if you stay put in today.

I am not just a teacher. Through the work of today, the tradition of tomorrow is built.

I am not just a teacher. "My interest is in the future because I will spend the rest of my life there." —C. F. Kettering

I am not just a teacher. A writer writes. If you want to be a writer, write.

I am not just a teacher. "Common sense is the collection of prejudices acquired by the age of eighteen." —Albert Einstein

I am not just a teacher. Privatization equals corruption.

I am not just a teacher. "I destroy my enemy by making him my friend." —Abe Lincoln

I am not just a teacher. "The moon lightens well but leaves certain areas in the dark." —an African proverb

I am not just a teacher. I am thankful for too much e-mail because it means I have friends who are thinking of me.

I am not just a teacher. Be loyal. Never pretend to be something you are not.

I am not just a teacher. When it comes to going after what you love in life, do not take no for an answer.

I am not just a teacher. When in doubt, you just take the next small step.

I am not just a teacher. Avoid biting when a simple growl will do.

I am not just a teacher. Let others know when they have invaded your territory.

I am not just a teacher. Overprepare, and then go with the flow.

I am not just a teacher. "History is the hand that pushes the future." —Unknown

I am not just a teacher. It is okay for your children to see you cry.

I am not just a teacher. Faith believes something is true in the absence of facts.

I am not just a teacher. Tomorrow is not promised to any of us.

I am not just a teacher. Luck is when opportunity meets preparation.

I am not just a teacher. The most important sex organ in your body is the brain.

I am not just a teacher. Growing old beats dying young.

I am not just a teacher. Believe in miracles.

I am not just a teacher. Read the bible for comfort, compassion, and energy.

I am not just a teacher. These children we teach only get one childhood. Make every day enjoyable and memorable.

I am not just a teacher. Without love, we have nothing.

I am not just a teacher. I have been part of many teams in my lifetime, but the very best team was then, and is now, the family.

I am not just a teacher. Great decisions are based on strong moral values taught in the family and reinforced by the life you live.

I am not just a teacher. Happy are those who have overcome their egos because teaching humbles you one, two, three seconds.

I am not just a teacher. "I commute all day and I am not going to commute all night long." —Johnny Carson

I am not just a teacher. Is not the word *lifetime* a powerful description of our legacy as voyeurs on this earth? We only have one, so make it count for something!

I am not just a teacher. "What luck for rulers that man does not think." —Adolf Hitler

I am not just a teacher. The Sunday school teacher asked, "Johnny, tell me, do you say prayers before eating?" He replied, "We do not have to. My mom is a good cook!"

I am not just a teacher. Little Bobby asked his grandmother how old she was. The grandmother answered, "Thirty-nine and holding." Little Bobby thought for a moment and then asked, "And how old would you be if you let go?"

I am not just a teacher. But I am taken back by the quiet grace and dignity of a cemetery.

I am not just a teacher. If life is a waste of time, and time is a waste of life, then let's all get wasted together and have the time of our lives.

I am not just a teacher. But beauty is just a light switch away.

I am not just a teacher. We cannot use the same yardstick to measure every student.

I am not just a teacher. The library is the only place where thousands of worlds wait quietly and patiently to be discovered.

I am not just a teacher. "You can't worry about what somebody else is doing. You come out and work hard every day. You play and let your performance speak for you. If things don't work out, at least you know you gave it everything you had." —Clif Groce

I am not just a teacher. You must have the look of love in your eyes.

I am not just a teacher. "The journey of one thousand miles starts with a single step." —Lao Tzu

I am not just a teacher. You need to claim the events of your life to make yourself you.

I am not just a teacher. Truth is always the strongest argument.

I am not just a teacher. Life is for sharing.

I am not just a teacher. I have experienced love, life, and loss. I am ready to experience love, laughter, and friendship again.

I am not just a teacher. Life is full of simple pleasures.

I am not just a teacher. I do not want to get to the end of my life and find that I just lived the length of it. I want to have lived the width of it also.

I am not just a teacher. Does smiling make others wonder what you are up to?

I am not just a teacher. "If your actions inspire others to dream more, learn more, do more, and become more, you are a leader." —John Quincy Adams

I am not just a teacher. "Be yourself; everyone else is taken." —Oscar Wilde

I am not just a teacher. "We do not stop playing because we grow old; we grow old and stop playing." —George Bernard Shaw

I am not just a teacher. Share the first smile of the day and the last embrace of the evening.

I am not just a teacher. Life is not a dress rehearsal.

I am not just a teacher. Don't wait for the storm to pass; learn to dance in the rain.

I am not just a teacher. Let's give them something to talk about.

I am not just a teacher. I would rather be hated for who I am than loved for who I am not.

I am not just a teacher. Happiness is an attitude.

I am not just a teacher. Laughter is the best medicine.

I am not just a teacher. Love is not just one thing; it is a million little things.

I am not just a teacher. It is what it is.

I am not just a teacher. "It's about dignity and self-esteem, which is not quite the same as vanity." —Randy Paulsh

I am not just a teacher. Come on in from the fog.

I am not just a teacher. The simplest pleasures are the truest treasures. Together is better.

I am not just a teacher. One plus one equals *everything*.

I am not just a teacher. Everyone has a place in the sun.

I am not just a teacher. I am not what happened to me. I am what I chose to become. —C. Jang

I am not just a teacher. Take a deep breath; it will calm you down.

I am not just a teacher. Envy is a waste of time.

I am not just a teacher: "This is the time for careful looking, for happy surprises. For reveling in the newness of things, when the entire world is fresh, and its freshness brings only joy." —Hubert Bermont, speaking of graduation from high school.

I am not just a teacher. "Education is a social process. Education is growth. Education is not preparation for life. Education is life itself." —John Dewey

I am not just a teacher. "Be faithful to that which exists nowhere but in yourself—and there make yourself indispensable." —Andre Gide

I am not just a teacher. "You not only have the right to be an individual; you have an obligation to be one. You cannot make any useful contribution in life unless you do this." —Eleanor Roosevelt

I am not just a teacher. "You will do foolish things, but do them with enthusiasm." —Colette

I am not just a teacher. "Oh, what a tangled web do parents weave when they think that their children are naïve." —Ogden Nash

I am not just a teacher. At the feast of egos, everyone leaves hungry.

I am not just a teacher. It is hard to make a comeback when you haven't been anywhere.

I am not just a teacher. Make love, not war. Hell, do both and get married.

I am not just a teacher. If *pro* is the opposite of *con*, then what is the opposite of *progress*? *Congress*!

I am not just a teacher, Married men live longer than single men do, but married men are a lot more willing to die.

I am not just a teacher. "I would rather be thought of as a teacher than a coach." —Bobby Knight

I am not just a teacher. But to be happy with a man, you must understand him a lot and love him a little. To be happy with a woman, you must love her a lot and not try to understand her at all.

I am not just a teacher. "Don't let what you cannot do interfere with what you can do." —John Wooden

I am not just a teacher But a woman always has the last word in an argument. Anything a man says after that is the beginning of a new argument.

I am not just a teacher. Old aunts used to come up to me at weddings, poking me in the ribs and cackling, telling me, "You're next." They stopped after I started doing the same thing to them at funerals.

I am not just a teacher. "An excuse is like a rocking chair. It keeps you going but gets you nowhere." —Unknown.

I am not just a teacher. Have you ever watched the sunrise and reminded yourself how today is a new opportunity for success and achievement?

I am not just a teacher. It is your fellow teachers who do you in, not the students.

I am not just a teacher. When I see, I remember. When I hear, I forget. When I do, I learn. This is the path I travel.

I am not just a teacher. Dreams, no matter how big or small, can come true anytime.

I am not just a teacher. A man falls in love with his eyes, and a woman with her ears.

I am not just a teacher. Death can never stop true love.

I am not just a teacher. Greatness on education can be passed on.

I am not just a teacher. Kindness is a virtue I admire.

I am not just a teacher. Sometimes the best things in life happen after you've done what you are supposed to do.

I am not just a teacher. A road less traveled. I believe everyone we meet influences us, be it elusive or tangible.

I am not just a teacher. "Life is an adventure or nothing at all." —Helen Keller

I am not just a teacher. Circumstances do not make the man, they reveal him.

I am not just a teacher. Just breathe!

I am not just a teacher. If you cannot laugh at yourself, who can you laugh at?

I am not just a teacher. Be kind and intellectually curious.

I am not just a teacher. What people say you cannot do, you try, and find out you can.

I am not just a teacher. I just want to dance.

I am not just a teacher. You are beautiful, but what else can you offer?

I am not just a teacher. Be the source of strength and courage.

I am not just a teacher. "Eighty percent of success is just showing up." —Woody Allen

I am not just a teacher. Here is to simplicity, sincerity, insight, and good music.

I am not just a teacher. Win today and walk together forever.

I am not just a teacher. If you can remember what it felt like to sit in a desk when you were a student in the grade level you teach, then do so.

I am not just a teacher. Put yourself into a famous picture. Now tell us how you feel.

I am not just a teacher. Tomorrow will be different—not necessarily better, but different.

I am not just a teacher. After teaching for forty years, are you cynical toward your students, or is it you just do not care?

I am not just a teacher. Be genuine to your beliefs.

I am not just a teacher. Body, mind, and spirit must be in sync with the universe to be a teacher.

I am not just a teacher. But I recognize that teaching is a work in progress.

I am not just a teacher. "In teaching, you cannot see the fruit of a day's work. It is invisible and remains so, maybe for twenty years." —Jacques Barzun

I am not just a teacher. A tidbit from Dr. Phil. Dr. Phil proclaimed, "The way to achieve inner peace is to finish all the things you started and never finished." So I looked around my house to see the things I started and had not finished. Before leaving the house this morning, I finished off a bottle of Merlot, a bottle of white Zinfandel, a bottle of Bailey's Irish cream, a bottle of Kahlua, a package of Oreos, the rest of my old Prozac prescription, the rest of the cheesecake, some Doritos, and a box of chocolates. You have no idea how good I feel!

I am not just a teacher. Yield to being cooperative when necessary and hold to your teaching ethics when necessary, but above all, know the difference.

I am not just a teacher. All that truly matters in the end is that you loved.

I am not just a teacher. Being correct may not be right!

I am not just a teacher. "I'll take my outstretched hand and offer it to anyone who comes along and tells me they are in need of love, in need of hope, or maybe just a friend." —Rod McKuen

I am not just teacher. We must live for today and dream for tomorrow.

I am not just a teacher. I have mentioned this before, but always show one exception to a commonly held myth, and it is exposed for what it is. Perception is reality. Well, if equality in corporate America was as perceived, we would have many more qualified minority individuals in decision-making positions. I wonder if that is perceived reality or just reality.

I am not just a teacher. If you do any work on the depression, may I recommend the showing of *Cinderella Man*, the story of boxer James J. Braddock. This is not just a boxing story, but a story of how strong family love and determination against the odds can persevere even through the worst economic times of the previous century. When I was doing a unit on the depression, I showed this film, and to my astonishment, not one student slept, talked, or fooled around. They were caught up in the story to the extent where you could hear a pin drop, and on occasion, I observed some of my students drying their eyes. Please show this movie and make a note to talk about family values and the relationships of parents to their children and husbands to wives.

I am not just a teacher. Did you know who Siddhartha Guatama is? He is Confucius.

I am not just a teacher. "I am not afraid of tomorrow, for I have seen yesterday, and I love today." —William Allen White

I am not just a teacher. "I am young, I am strong and living a great adventure." —Anne Frank.

I am not just a teacher. The most important human trait I teach is strength. Not physical strength but strength of character because that is what makes the difference in the human spirit that develops the total person.

I am not just a teacher. Have you ever explained to your son or daughter why they possess the name you gave them? Understanding the human identity is gateway to the human's growth.

I am not just a teacher. Have you ever wanted to do something but you did not? Well, today I made a contribution to the Dana Farber Cancer Institute in Boston in the name of my father, John. I would be a remiss if I did not say that, after all of these years, whenever I think of my dad, I still get a lump in my throat and tears in my eyes because of the love I had for him and the suffering he endured. He had tons of guts and strength and he, like my mom, will always be in my mind and heart because they are my true heroes.

I am not just a teacher. "What lies behind us and what lies before us are tiny matters compared to what lies within us." —Ralph Waldo Emerson

I am not just a teacher. We don't receive wisdom. "We must discover it for ourselves after a journey that no one can take for us or spare us." —Marcel Proust

I am not just a teacher. "Wear a smile and have friends, wear a frown, and have wrinkles." —George Eliot

I am not just a teacher. The days of Camelot are behind us. We must prepare the next generation of leaders in our public schools, colleges, and universities.

I am not just a teacher. Cut education = cut dreams.

I am not just a teacher. Cut potential = encourage despair.

I am not just a teacher. To achieve is a destination of the mind, body, and soul of a person.

I am not just a teacher. A teacher helps you achieve the future you thought you could only imagine.

I am not just a teacher. What will your expectation be next?

I am not just a teacher. Master your craft and then expand your horizons.

I am not just a teacher. Imagine a brighter future.

I am not just a teacher. Fear is not a way to live or die.

I am not just a teacher. Is dissent the highest form of patriotism?

I am not just a teacher. "The possibility that we may fail in the struggle ought not to deter us from the support of the cause we believe in to be just." —Abraham Lincoln

I am not just a teacher. We are the gatekeepers of education and the moral think tanks for generations yet to come.

I am not just a teacher. "A teacher affects eternity. He/she can never tell where their influence stops." —Unknown

I am not just a teacher. "You cannot build a reputation on what you are going to do." —Henry Ford

I am not just a teacher. "But don't we lie loudest when we lie to ourselves?" —Eric Huffer

I am not just a teacher. "Obstacles are those things you see when you take your eyes off the goal." —Henry Ford

I am not just a teacher. Listen, if you are worried about what your legacy is going to be in life, you need not look any further than how you prepared your children to take their places in society. If you taught them about life, people, governments, humanity, and let them make mistakes in judgments—you have nothing to worry about. I am very proud—no, exceptionally proud—of my sons.

I am not just a teacher: You can retire to the Deep South where you can rent a movie and buy bait in the same store; "y'all" is singular, and "y'all" is plural; "he needed killin'" is a valid defense; everyone has two names: Billy Bob, Jimmy Bob, Mary Sue, Betty Jean, Mary Beth, etc.; everything is either "in yonder," "over yonder," or "out yonder." It is important to know the difference too.

I am not just a teacher. Teaching is a profession dealing in the immeasurable results conducted through invisible processes with an inconclusive audience. In short, an act of faith.

I am not just a teacher. As long as the world continues to change, so can societies all over the world.

I am not just a teacher. The pursuit of the difficult makes us strong.

I am not just a teacher. "Excellence is the gradual result of always striving to do better." —Pat Riley

I am not just a teacher. "I missed more than nine thousand shots in my career. I've lost almost three hundred games. Twenty-six times I've been trusted to take the game winning shot and missed. I've failed over and over again in my life. And that is why I succeed." —Michael Jordan

I am not just a teacher. Love is the speed of light.

I am not just a teacher. It is your faults that make you real.

I am not just a teacher. My classroom is education. Put passion in action.

I am not just a teacher. Fifth-grade friendship can divide a cookie more accurately than a fifth-grade math exercise.

I am not just a teacher. Adversity comes to pass, not to stay.

I am not just a teacher. Every *no* brings you closer to a *yes*.

I am not just a teacher. We do what we have to do, to do what we want to do.

I am not just a teacher. Love lives on in the little things you shared, in the moments you will always treasure, in the smiles you can never forget.

I am not just a teacher. Champions belong to the ages.

I am not just a teacher. Set goals in the following areas: religion, family, job, friends.

I am not just a teacher. You have to learn before you can lead.

I am not just a teacher. A classroom, like love, is built one day at a time. And it takes patience, honesty, passion, compromise, and the ability to grow.

I am not just a teacher. "But whatever you fear, go there." —Billie Jean King

I am not just a teacher. No truth is ever a lie!

I am not just a teacher. "We are what we repeatedly do. Excellence then is not and art, but a habit." —Aristotle

I am not just a teacher. Ever been weary enough to quit? Where do we find the courage to continue?

I am not just a teacher. Bring your students into your teaching world and let them see the possibilities. Do not be dragged into their worlds.

I am not just a teacher. Do not make excuses, make a difference.

I am not just a teacher. Remember when this economic crisis of 2008–2009 hit, and congress let Bear Sterns go under, pushed a bunch of forced marriages between banks? They bailed out AIG. At the time, most people asked, "What does an insurance company have to do with this financial crisis?" The answer is simple: AIG insures the pension trust of the United States Congress! No wonder they got bailed out first.

I am not just a teacher. When you move beyond your dreams and achieve success, you finally become free.

I am not just a teacher. You can retire to Maine where you only have four spices: salt, pepper, ketchup, and Tabasco; Halloween costumes fit over parkas; you have more than one recipe for moose; sexy lingerie is anything flannel with less than eight buttons; the four seasons are winter, still winter, almost winter, and construction.

I am not just a teacher. A man without a woman is like a river without a source.

I am not just a teacher. Love is a covenant that we build on a strong foundation, and that is why we do not develop it within a day.

I am not just a teacher. "When you get to the end of your rope, tie a knot and hold on." —Franklin Delano Roosevelt

I am not just a teacher. But doesn't attitude reflect leadership?

I am not just a teacher. But if it is a Monday morning, you pretty much know what kind of a day is coming.

I am not just a teacher. Always protect democracy because power corrupts, and absolute power corrupts absolutely.

I am not just a teacher. A true friend is someone who reaches for your hand and touches your heart.

I am not just a teacher. The happiest people don't have the best of everything; they simply make the best of everything. So live simply, love generously, care deeply, speak kindly, and above all else, enjoy your coffee.

I am not just a teacher. "But you cannot enjoy swimming if you don't get your feet wet." —Homer J.

I am not just a teacher. "We must live so that, when we die, even the undertaker will feel sorry." —Bill Matthews

I am not just a teacher. "I've learned that regretting the past is a waste of time; learn from it instead." —Chavo

I am not just a teacher. Memory is a magnet. It will pull to it and hold only material nature has designed it to attract.

I am not just a teacher. I've learned that you shouldn't go through life with a catcher's mitt on both hands. You need to be able to throw something back.

I am not just a teacher. I've learned that if you pursue happiness, it will elude you. But if you focus on your family, your friends, the needs of others, your work, and doing the very best you can, happiness will find you.

I am not just a teacher. I've learned that whenever I decide something with an open heart, I usually make the right decision.

I am not just a teacher. To avoid criticism, do nothing, say nothing, and be nothing.

I am not just a teacher. But there was a man sunbathing naked at the beach. For the sake of civility, and to keep it from getting sunburned, he had his hat over his privates. A woman walks past and says, snickering, "If you were a gentleman, you'd lift your hat." He raised an eyebrow and replied, "If you weren't so ugly, it would lift itself."

I am not just a teacher. That every day you should reach out and touch someone. People love that human touch—holding hands, a warm hug, or a friendly pat on the back.

I am not just a teacher. But I have learned that I still have a lot to learn.

I am not just a teacher. If I cannot change, how can I expect my students to change?

I am not just a teacher. Learning is how to teach.

I am not just a teacher. Your zeal and emotion for teaching is evergreen.

I am not just a teacher. But teaching is loyalty, respect, and meaning in your everyday life so you can lead by example.

I am not just a teacher. Teaching is like being a divorced parent with thirty-two children to love, care for, oversee, and guide along the path of literacy.

I am not just a teacher. It is a very good thing for our sanity and self-esteem that we cannot always correctly read either people's faces or minds.

I am not just a teacher. "Celebrate we will because life is short but sweet for certain." —The Dave Matthews Band

I am not just a teacher. My mind not only wanders; it sometimes leaves completely.

I am not just a teacher. The nice thing about living in a small town is that when you do not know what you are doing, someone else will.

I am not just a teacher. Just when I was getting used to yesterday, along came today.

I am not just a teacher. Sometimes I think I understand everything, and then I regain consciousness.

I am not just a teacher. The trouble with some women is that they get all excited about nothing, and then they marry him.

I am not just a teacher. There are five rules for a happy life: 1) it's important to have a woman who helps at home, who cooks from time to time, cleans up, and has a job; 2) it's important to have a woman who can make you laugh; 3) it's important to have a woman you can trust and does not lie to you; 4) it's important to have a woman who is good in bed and likes to be with you; 5) it's very, very important that these four women do not know each other.

I am not just a teacher. Nothing lasts forever, so make the most of being a paid professional.

I am not just a teacher. True love fills your heart with meaning and devotion because it has two remembrances, the heart and the mind.

I am not just a teacher. Once you have made a decision, never look back and never ask what if because it will weaken your resolve.

I am not just a teacher. But I would love to fly in space.

I am not just a teacher. The kingdom of God is inside all of you. Use it!

I am not just a teacher. Most people have one chance at being great. Do it!

I am not just a teacher. Heroes get remembered; legends never die.

I am not just a teacher. Follow your heart, you can never go wrong.

I am not just a teacher. Is forever a long time?

I am not just a teacher. North Quincy High School in Quincy, Massachusetts, has produced three Congressional Medal of Honor winners, and the air force pilot who dropped the atomic bomb on Hiroshima. What does that say about the type of character and devotion to duty they learned in a public school?

I am not just a teacher. Feeling stupid is good for a body.

I am not just a teacher. The more you say yes, the more variety there is in you your life.

I am not just a teacher. Loved ones never die; they live in your heart for eternity.

I am not just a teacher. "Always acknowledge your faults. This will throw those in authority off their guard and give you an opportunity to commit more." —Mark Twain

I am not just a teacher. A woman can bring emotion from a man with a look, a word, or a touch.

I am not just a teacher. Albert Einstein once said, "Insanity is defined as doing the same thing over and over again and expecting different results."

I am not just a teacher. "It is better to drink this beer and let their dreams come true than be selfish and worry about my liver." —George Herman "Babe" Ruth

I am not just a teacher. "Nobody talks of entrepreneurship as survival, but that's exactly what it is." —Anita Roddick

I am not just a teacher. "A friendship founded on business is a good deal better than a business founded on friendship." —John D. Rockefeller

I am not just a teacher. "Make each day your masterpiece. You have control over that." —John Wooden

I am not just a teacher. "You cannot win a battle in any arena merely by defending yourself." —President Richard Nixon

I am not just a teacher. "You miss 100 percent of the shots you never take." —Wayne Gretsky

I am not just a teacher. "To be successful in anything, a person must always want to be better, not only than your opponent but better than your last performance. Done correctly, being competitive is a wonderful way to always try to be a better person by learning from your mistakes and capitalizing on your successes." —Hale Erwin

I am not just a teacher. "The wonderful thing about the game of life is that winning and losing are only temporary—unless you quit." —Unknown

I am not just a teacher. "Success isn't something that just happens—success is learned, practiced, and then it is shared." —Sparky Anderson

I am not just a teacher. "Nobody who gave their best effort has ever regretted it." —George Halas

I am not just a teacher. "If a team is to reach its potential, each player must willingly subordinate his/her own personal goals to the good of the team." —Bud Wilkinson

I am not just a teacher. "Last season, we could not win at home, and this season we can't win on the road. My failure as a coach is that I can't think of anyplace else to play." —Harry Neale

I am not just a teacher. Do not live your life like a raindrops that weave their weary paths and die, rather find meaning to your life's pursuits and live it to the fullest.

I am not just a teacher. "It's easy to get players. Getting them to play together, that's the hard part." —Casey Stengel

This Makes You Think a Bit

The light turned yellow, just in front of him. He did the right thing, stopping at the crosswalk, even though he could have beaten the light by accelerating through the intersection.

The tailgating woman was furious and honked her horn, screaming in frustration, as she missed her chance to get through the intersection, dropping her cell phone and makeup. As she was still in mid-rant, she heard a tap on her window and looked up into the face of a very serious police officer. The officer ordered her to exit her car with her hands up.

He took her to the police station where she was searched, fingerprinted, photographed, and placed in a holding cell. After a couple of hours, a policeman approached the cell and opened the door. She was escorted to the booking desk where the arresting officer was waiting with her personal effects.

He said, "I am very sorry for this mistake. You see, I pulled up behind your car while you were blowing your horn, flipping off the guy in front of you, and cussing a blue streak at him. I noticed the 'What would Jesus do' bumper sticker, the 'choose life' license plate holder, the 'follow me to Sunday school' bumper sticker, and the chrome-plated Christian fish emblem on the trunk, so naturally, I assumed you had stolen the car."

Priceless!

Silly Things You Need to Know

If you yelled for eight years, seven months, and six days, you would have produced enough sound energy to heat one cup of coffee.

If you farted consistently for six years and nine months, enough gas is produced to create the energy of an atomic bomb.

The human heart created enough pressure when it pumps out of the body to squirt blood over thirty feet. OMG!

A pig's orgasm lasts thirty minutes. (In my next life, I want to be a pig.)

A cockroach will live nine days without its head before it starves to death. (I am still not over the pig.)

Banging your head against a wall uses 150 calories an hour.

A male praying mantis cannot copulate while its head is attached to its body. The female initiates sex by ripping the male's head off.

And God Created Teachers

God created the world and then…

On the sixth day, God created men and women.

On the seventh day, he rested.

Not so much to recuperate, but rather to prepare himself for the work he was going to do on the next day. For it was on that day, the eighth day, that God created *the first teacher*.

The *teacher*, though taken from among men and women, had several significant modifications. In general, God made the teacher more durable than other men and women. The teacher was made to arise at a very early hour and to go to bed no earlier than 11:30 p.m. with no rest in between.

The teacher had to be able to withstand being locked up in airtight classroom for six hours with thirty-five monsters on a rainy Monday. And the teacher had to be fit to correct 103 term papers over Easter vacation.

Yes, God made the teacher tough but gentle too. The teacher was equipped with soft hands to wipe away the tears of the neglected, lonely student; those of a sixteen-year-old girl who was not asked to the prom.

And into the teacher, God poured a generous amount of patience. Patience when a student asks to repeat the directions the teacher has just repeated for someone else. Patience when the kids forget their lunch money for the fourth day in a row. Patience when one-third of the class fails a test. Patience when the textbooks have not arrived yet, and the school year starts tomorrow.

And God gave the teacher a heart slightly bigger than the average human heart. For the teacher's heart had to be big enough to love the kid who screams, "I hate this class. It is boring!" And to love the kid who runs out of the classroom at the end of the period without so much as a "good-bye," let alone a "thank you."

And, lastly, God gave the teacher an abundant supply of hope. For God knows that the teacher would always be hoping. Hoping that kids would someday learn how to spell, hoping not to have lunchroom duty, hoping that Friday would come, hoping for a free day, and hoping for deliverance.

When God finished creating the teacher, he stepped back and admired the work of his hands. And God saw the teacher was good. Very good! And because God loves teachers so much, on the ninth day, God created "snow days."

No Parent Left Behind

I am not just a teacher. But wouldn't you like to look at some of the notes my fellow professionals received across this great country of ours? And then maybe you will be left to ponder who really has been left behind by George W. Bush.

- My son is under a doctor's care and should not take PE today. Please execute him.
- Please excuse Lisa for being absent. She was sick, and I had her shot.
- Dear school, please excuse John for being absent on January 26, 29, 30, 31, 32, and also 33.
- Please excuse Gloria from *jim* today. She is administrating.
- Please excuse Roland from PE for a few days. Yesterday, he fell out of a tree and misplaced his hip.
- Carlos was absent yesterday because he was playing football and got hurt in a growth part.
- Megan could not come to school today because she has been bothered by very close veins.
- Please excuse Ray Friday from school. He has very loose vowels.
- Please excuse Pedro from being absent yesterday. He had (diahre, dyrea, dieathe) *the shits*. (Note: the words in the parentheses were crossed out).
- Irving was absent yesterday because he missed his bust.
- Please excuse Bill for being absent. It was his father's fault.
- Sally won't be in school a week from Friday. We have to attend her funeral.

- My daughter was absent yesterday because she was tired. She spent a weekend with the marines.
- Please excuse Jason for being absent yesterday. He had a cold and could not breed well.
- Please excuse Brenda. She has been sick and under the doctor.
- Maryann, Jane, and Elsie was absent on December 11–16 with a sore throat, headache, and upset stomach. I wasn't the best either with a sore throat and fever. There must be something going around, her father was hot last night.
- Please excuse Mary for being absent yesterday. She was in bed with Gramps.

My Letter to the World

by Samantha Brier

When I was born, you embraced me with a warmth and understanding
I will never know again.
You have taught me lessons after lesson,
You have left me out in the cold,
Lashed out at me and beat me till I could not see a light at the end of
    the tunnel.
You have spat on me and called me hurtful names.
Numerous times, you have even kicked me when I was down,
But I am still here,
Not to fight you nor to get in your face, but to tell you something:
I *won*!

Yes, I know I have done wrong,
I also know you have done the same.
But there is one thing you need to know:
I am a person.
I hurt, I think, I cry, I feel.
I am who I am
You are who you are.
I have never walked in your shoes, and you would get lost in mine,

For the life you handed me so long, aged with graceful arms,
Is full of ups and downs,
Roads that wind and mountains to climb.
No longer will I listen to your words of doubt nor will I be there for
    you to push around.

You see, my whole life I have tried to have you accept me
But I have come to accept myself, to love me for who I am
And that is all I really need.

Sit back, relax, and watch me turn all of my dreams into reality.

I Am Enough

I am enough, just as I am,
Unfinished,
Imperfect,
Uncertain of the road I choose,
Yet certain that I must continue.

I cannot go back.
I am not enough for some,
And too much for others.

I struggle with myself,
I wrestle with my fears,
I avoid the parts of me
That are dark and unavoidable.

Yet I want to hide no more,
I am alive,
I know because I feel.

In my eyes, I am
Damaged,
Hurting,
Healing,
In need of improvement.

But in the eyes of God,
And in the place where grace abides,
I know I am enough.

The Primitive History

From the Book of Genesis:

In the beginning, God created the heavens and the earth;
The earth was a waste and void;
Darkness covered the abyss,
And the spirit of God was stirring above the waters.

God said, "Let there be light," and there was light.
God saw the light was good.
God separated the light from darkness,
Calling the light *day* and
The darkness, *night*.

Don't Quit

When things go wrong, as they sometimes will
When the road you're trudging seems all uphill,
When the funds are low and the debts are high,
And you want to smile, but you have to sigh,
When care is pressing you down a bit,
Rest if you must, but don't quit.

Life is queer with its twists and turns,
As everyone of us sometimes learns, and many a failure turns about,
When he/she might have won had he stuck it out;
Don't give up though the pace seems slow,
You may success with another blow.

Success is failure turned inside out,
The solver tint of the clouds of doubt,
And you never can tell how close you are,
It may be near when it seems far;
So stick to the fight when it seems so far;
So stick to the fight when you are hardest hit,
It's when things seem worse,
That you must not quit.

My Sweet Rose

The first day of schools, our professor introduced himself and challenged us to get to know someone we did not already know. I stood up to looked around when a gentle hand touched my shoulder. I turned around to find a wrinkled little old lady beaming up at me with a smile that lit up her entire being.

She said, "Hi, handsome. My name is Rose. I am eighty-seven years old. Can I give you a hug?"

I laughed and enthusiastically responded, "Of course you may!" And she gave me a giant squeeze.

"Why are you in college at such a young, innocent age?" I asked.

She jokingly replied, "I'm here to meet a rich husband, get married, and have a couple of kids."

"No, seriously," I asked. I was curious what may have motivated her to be taking on this challenge at her age.

"I always dreamed of having a college education, and now I am getting one!" she told me.

After class, we walked to the student union building and shared a chocolate milkshake. We became instant friends. Every day for the next three months, we would leave class together and talk nonstop. I was always mesmerized listening to this "time machine" as she shared her wisdom and experience with me.

Over the course of the year, Rose became a campus icon, and she easily made friends wherever she went. She loved to dress up, and she reveled in the attention bestowed upon her by the other students. She was living it up.

At the end of semester, we invited Rose to speak at our football banquet. I'll never forget what she taught us. She was introduced, and she stepped up to the podium. As she began to deliver her prepared speech, she dropped her three-by-five cards on the floor. Frustrated and a little embarrassed, she leaned into the microphone and simply said, "I'm sorry I'm so jittery. I gave up beer for lent, and this whiskey is killing me! I'll never get my speech back in order, so let me just tell you what I know." As we laughed, she cleared her throat and began, "We do not stop playing because we are old. We grow old because we stop playing."

There are four secrets to staying young, being happy, and achieving success: you have to laugh and find humor in every day; you have got to have a dream; when you lose dreams, you die; we have so many people walking around who are dead and do not even know it!

There is a huge difference between growing older and growing up. If you are nineteen years old and lie in bed for a year and do not do one productive thing, you will turn twenty years old. If I am eighty-seven years old and stay in bed for a year and never do anything, I will turn eighty-eight. Anybody can grow older. That does not take any talent or ability. The idea is to grow up by finding opportunity in change. Have no regrets.

"The elderly usually do not have any regrets for what we did, but rather for things we did not do. The only people who fear death are those with regrets."

She concluded her speech by courageously singing "The Rose." She challenged each of us to study the lyrics and live them out in our daily lives. At the year's end, Rose finished the college degree she had begun all those years ago.

One week after graduation, Rose died peacefully in her sleep. Over two thousand college students attended the funeral in tribute to the wonderful woman who taught by example that it is never too late to be all you can possibly be.

These words have been passed along in loving memory of Rose: "Remember, growing older is mandatory. Growing up is optional. We make a living by what we get; we make a life by what we give. God

71

promises a safe landing, not a calm passage. If God brings you to it, he will bring you through it."

Good friends are like stars… you do not always see them, but you know they are always there for you.

This is a tribute to all the teachers who hang in there every day.
You might be employed by a school if

1. You believe the playground should be equipped with a Ritalin salt lick.
2. You want to slap the next person who says, "Must be nice to work eight to three thirty and have your summers off.
3. You can tell it's a full moon without ever looking outside.
4. You believe "shallow gene pool" should have its own box on the report card.
5. You believe that unspeakable evils will befall you if anyone says, "Boy, the kids are quiet today."
6. When out in public, you feel the urge to snap your fingers at children you do not know and correct their behavior.
7. You have no social life between August and June.
8. Marking all *A*s on report cards would make your life so much easier.
9. You think people should be required to get a government permit before being allowed to reproduce.
10. You wonder how some parents managed to reproduced. Amazing!
11. You laugh uncontrollably when people refer to the staff room as a lounge.
12. You encourage an obnoxious parent to check into charter schools or home schools.

13. You can't have children because there's no name you can give your child that would not bring on high blood pressure the moment you heard it uttered.

14. You think caffeine should be available in an intravenous form.

15. You know you are in for a major project when a parent says, "I have a great idea I'd like to discuss. I think it would be such fun."

16. Meeting a child's parent instantly answers the question, "Why is this child like this?"

Sports Quotes

Beyond life and family, baseball is the most important aspect of my life, as it has helped shape my values, mind, body, and soul.

They say it can't be done, but that doesn't always work. —Casey Stengel

When you watch baseball at its best, there's a tendency to forget the real world. —Mickey Mantle

Make optimism a way of life. —Brooks Robinson

If you are afraid, you'll never do the job. —Bill Mazeroski

You gotta believe. —Tug McGraw

There's a good kind of ignorance. Sometimes you're just too dumb to know you can't do the impossible. —Joe Garagiola

Never let the fear of striking out get in your way. —Babe Ruth

Experience is a tough teacher. It gives the test before presenting the lesson. —Vern Law

To play ball was what I lived for. I used to like to play so much that I loved to take infield practice. I hated it when we got rained out. —Mickey Mantle

It is essential to understand that battles are primarily won in the hearts of men. —Vince Lombardi

Failures are expected by losers, ignored by winners. —Joe Gibbs

I believe in discipline. You can forgive incompetence. You can forgive lack of ability. But one thing you cannot forgive is the lack of discipline. — Forrest Gregg

I consider skateboarding an art form, a lifestyle, and a sport. —Tony Hawk

Swing hard, in case they throw the ball where you're swinging. —Duke Snider

Failure is not fatal, but failure to change might be. —John Wooden

The game isn't over until it's over. —Yogi Berra

The secret of winning football games is working more as a team and less as individuals. I play not my eleven best, but my best eleven. —Knute Rockne

Free your mind, and the rest will follow. —En Vogue

Just a Little Boy

by Bob Fox
(former Minor League pitcher)

He stands at the plate with heart
Pounding fast.

The bases are loaded; the die has been cast.
Mom and Dad cannot help him, he stands
All alone.

A hit at this moment would send the
Team home.

The ball meets the plate; he swings and
He misses.

There's a groan from the crowd, with
Some boos and some hisses.

A thoughtless voice cries, "Strike out
The bum."

Tears fill his eyes; the game's no longer fun.
So open your heart and give him a break.

For it's moments like this, a man can make.
Keep this in mind when you hear someone forget.

He's just a little boy, and not a man yet.

Shay

Author Unknown

At a fundraising dinner for a school that serves learning-disabled children, the father of one of the students delivered a speech that would never be forgotten by all who attended

"When not interfered with by outside influences, everything nature does is done with perfection. Yet my son, Shay, cannot learn things as other children do. He cannot understand things as other children do. Where is the natural order of things in my son?"

The audience was stilled by the query. The father continued. "I believe that when a child like Shay, physically and mentally handicapped, comes into the world, an opportunity to realize true human nature presents itself, and it comes, in the way other people treat that child."

Then he told the following story:

Shay and his father had walked past a park where some boys Shay knew were playing baseball. Shay asked, "Do you think they will let me play?"

Shay's father knew that most of the boys would not want someone like Shay on their team, but the father also understood that if his son were allowed to play, it would give him a much-needed sense of belonging and some confidence to be accepted by others in spite of his handicaps.

Shay's father approached one of the boys on the field and asked if Shay could play, not expecting much. The boy looked around for guidance, and a few of the boys nodded approval, *why not?* So he took matters into his own hands and said, "We're losing by six runs, and the game is in the eighth inning. I guess he can be on our team, and we'll try to put him in to bat in the ninth inning."

Shay struggled over to the team's bench, put on a team shirt with a broad smile, and his father had a small tear in his eye and warmth in his heart. The boys saw the father's joy at his son being accepted.

In the bottom of the eighth inning, Shay's team scored a few runs but was still behind by three. In the top of the ninth inning, Shay put on a glove and played right field. Even though no hits came his way, he was obviously ecstatic just to be in the game and on the field, grinning from ear to ear as his father waved to him from the stands.

In the bottom of the ninth inning, Shay's team scored again. Now, with two outs and the bases loaded, the potential winning run was on base, and Shay was scheduled to be next at bat.

At this juncture, do they let Shay bat and give away their chance to win the game? Surprisingly, Shay was given an at bat. Everyone knew that a hit was all, but it was impossible because Shay didn't even know how to hold the bat properly, much less connect with the ball.

However, Shay stepped up to the plate, the pitcher, recognizing the other team putting winning aside for *this* moment in Shay's life, moved in a few steps to lob the ball in softly so that Shay could at least be able to make contact.

The first pitch came, and Shay swung clumsily and missed. The pitcher again took a few steps forward to toss the ball softly toward Shay. As the pitch came in, Shay swung at the ball and hit a slow ground ball right back at the pitcher.

The game would now be over, but the pitcher picked up the soft ground ball and could have easily thrown the ball to the first baseman. Shay would have been out and that would have been the end of the game. Instead, the pitcher threw the ball right over the head of the first baseman, out of reach of all his teammates.

Everyone from the stands and both teams started yelling, "Shay, run to first! Run to first!" Never in his life had Shay ever ran that far, but he made it to first base.

He scampered down the baseline, wide-eyed and startled. Everyone yelled, "Run to second, run to second!" Catching his breath, Shay awkwardly ran toward second, gleaming and struggling to make it to second base.

By the time Shay started toward second base, the right fielder had the ball—the smallest guy on their team who had a chance to be a hero for his team for the first time. He could have thrown the ball to the second baseman for the tag, but he understood the pitcher's intentions, and he too, intentionally threw the ball high and far over the third baseman's head.

Shay ran toward second base deliriously as the runners ahead of him circled the bases toward home. All were screaming, "Shay, Shay. Shay, all the way, Shay."

As Shay reached second base, the opposing shortstop ran to help him and turned him in the direction of third base, shouting, "Run to third! Shay, run to third."

As Shay rounded third, the boys from both teams and those who were watching were on their feet, screamed, "Shay, run home."

Shay ran home, stepped on the plate, and was cheered as the hero who hit the "grand slam" and won the game for his team.

"That day," said the father softly, with tears now rolling down his face, "the boys from both teams helped bring a piece of true love and humanity into this world."

Shay did not make it to another summer and died that winter, having never forgotten being the hero making his father so happy, and coming home and seeing his mother tearfully embrace her little hero of the day!

God Is...

by Fifth-grade Students

A fifth-grade teacher in a Christian school asked her class to look at TV commercials and see if they could use them in some way to communicate ideas about God.

God is like Bayer aspirin; he works miracles.

God is like a Ford; he's got a better idea.

God is like Coke; he is the real thing.

God is like Hallmark cards; he cares enough to send his very best.

God is like Tide; he gets the stains out that other leave behind.

God is like General Electric; he brings good things to life.

God is like Sears; he has everything.

God is like Alka-Seltzer; try him, you'll like him.

God is like Scotch Tape; you can't see him, but you know he is there.

God is like Delta; he's ready when you are.

God is like Allstate; you're in good hands with him.

God is like VO-5 hair spray; he holds you through all kinds of weather.

God is like Dial soap; aren't you glad you have him? Don't you wish everybody did?

God is like the U.S. post office; neither rain nor snow nor sleet nor ice could keep him from his appointed destination.

You just might be a Blue Neck if

- You think a *barbecue* is a verb meaning, "to cook outside."
- You think Heinz ketchup is *really* spicy!
- You do not have any problem pronouncing *Worcestershire sauce* correctly.
- For breakfast, you would prefer *potato au gratin* to grits.
- You have never ever eaten okra, fried or boiled.
- You eat fried chicken with a knife and fork.
- You have no idea what a polecat is.
- You do not see anything wrong with putting a sweater on a poodle.
- You do not have bangs.
- You would rather have your son grow up to be a lawyer than to get his own TV fishing show.
- Instead of referring to two or more people as "y'all," "you guys," even if both of them are women.
- You never planned your summer vacation around a gun-n-knife show.
- You think more money should go to more important scientific research at your university than to pay the head football coach's salary.
- None of your fur coats are homemade.
- You do not have doilies, and you do not know how to make one.
- You can do your laundry without quarters.
- You get freaked out when people on the subway talk to you.

- You would never wear pink or appliqué sweatshirt.
- You call binoculars opera glasses.
- You cannot spit out the window without pulling over to the side of the road and stopping.
- You do not have hats in your closet that advertise feed stores.

Natural Highs

1. Falling in love
2. Laughing so hard it hurts
3. A hot shower
4. No lines at the supermarket
5. A special glance
6. Getting mail
7. Taking a drive on a scenic road
8. Hearing your favorite song on the radio
9. Hearing the voices that time stilled in your mind
10. Hot towels fresh out of the dryer
11. Chocolate milkshake or vanilla or strawberry
12. A bubble bath
13. Giggling
14. A good conversation
15. Feeling the mist touch your skin on a brilliant sunny day
16. Finding a twenty-dollar bill in your winter jacket
17. Laughing at yourself
18. Midnight phone calls that last for hours
19. Running through sprinklers
20. Laughing for absolutely no reason at all
21. Having someone tell you that you are beautiful
22. Laughing at an inside joke
23. Friends
24. Accidentally overhearing someone say something nice about you

25. Waking up and realizing you still have a few hours left to sleep
26. Your very first kiss
27. Making new friends or spending time with old ones
28. Holding your son or daughter for the very first time
29. Having someone play with your hair
30. Sweet dreams
31. Road trips with friends
32. Making eye contact with a cute stranger
33. Swinging on swings
34. Holding hands with someone you care about and feeling a small chill go up your spine and then down
35. Running into an old friend and realizing that some things never change
36. Watching the expression on someone's face as they open a much-desired present from you
37. Watching the sunrise and remembering things about your life you thought you had forgotten
38. Getting out of bed every day and being grateful for another day
39. Knowing that someone misses you
40. Getting a hug from some you deeply care about
41. Knowing you have done the right thing, no matter what other people think

A Story

by G. R. Romano

It was late one Tuesday evening,
Before a mother could sit down,
To tell her only child about
The terror that hit downtown.
She looked into the eyes of her son.
God, she loved him so much,
She felt her heart begin to break,
And the hurt began to show.

She gathered all her strength and courage,
As her story she began to tell,
"Baby, do not cry, but I'm afraid Daddy
Might be under the building that fell."

The boy looked back at his mother,
His eyes made not one blink,
And the mother's tears began to fall.
What would her baby think?

You see, his dad is a firefighter,
And his hero from the day of birth.
He loved his dad more than anything else
That could ever inherit this earth.

The mother's head began to drop,
Her forehead resting on her palm,
She thought her son would be upset,
Instead, he was very calm.

The boy leaned over towards his mom,
And put his hand on her head,
In her ear, he began to whisper,
And this is what he said:

"Mommy, please do not cry, I knew Daddy was not coming home.
I talked with him a while ago, but it wasn't on the phone.
He told me that he loved me,
And promised we would meet again,
He told me of his new home,
And the job he was to begin.

God is building an army,
And there are many angels needed,
That is where Daddy and the others went,
They weren't all defeated."

It was then the mother lifted her head,
The tears streamed down her face,
And she could feel her husband's presence,
As it filled her heart with grace.

It was then she knew her son was right,
He was in God's army now,
She also knew her son was safe,
That he'd be kept from harm somehow.

So evil doers of the world beware,
An army is on the way,
Bolstered by new angels,
Who left the towers that day.

Their commander has never been beaten,
His power has never been matched.
And if evil thinks he was almighty before…
Well, the surface has just been scratched.

God bless America!

If I Knew

If I knew it should be the last time
That I'd see you fall asleep,
I would tuck you in more lightly
And pray the Lord, your soul to keep.

If I knew it should be the last time
That I'd see you walk out the door,
I should give you a hug and a kiss
And call you back for one more.

If I knew it should be the last time
I'd hear your voice lifted up in praise,
I would video tape each action and word
As I could play them back day after day.

If I knew it would be the last time,
I should spare an extra minute
To stop and say, "I love you,"
Instead of assuming you should know I do.

If I knew it should be the last time,
I would be there to share your day.
Well, I'm sure you'll have so many more,
As I can let just this one slip away.

For surely there is always a tomorrow
To make up for an oversight,
And we always get a second chance
To make everything right.

There will always be another day
To say, "I love you,"
And certainly there's another chance
To say, "Anything I can do?"

Tomorrow is not promised to anyone,
Young or old alike,
And today may be their last chance
You get to hold your loved one tight.

So hold your loved ones close today,
And whisper in their ear.
Tell them how much you love them,
And that you'll always hold them dear.

Once a Jerk

A United States solider was attending some college courses between assignments. He had completed missions in Iraq and Afghanistan. One of the courses had a professor who was an avowed atheist and a member of the ACLU.

One day, the professor shocked the class when he came in. He looked to the ceiling and flatly stated, "God, if you are real, then I want you to knock me off this platform. I will give you fifteen minutes."

The lecture room fell silent. You could hear a pin drop. Ten minutes went by, and the professor proclaimed, "Here I am, God. I'm still waiting." It got down to the last couple of minutes when the solider got out of his chair, went up to the professor, and cold-cocked him, knocking him off the platform. The professor was out cold.

The solider went back to his seat and sat there, silently. The other students were shocked and stunned and sat there, looking on in silence.

The professor eventually came to, noticeably shaken, looked at the solider and asked, "What the hell is the matter with you? Why did you do that?"

The solider calmly replied, "God was too busy today protecting America's soldiers who are protecting your right to say stupid shit and act like an asshole. So he sent me."

A Thousand Marbles

The older I get, the more I enjoy Saturday mornings. Perhaps it's the quiet solitude that comes with being the first to rise, or maybe it's the unbounded joy of not having to be at work. Either way, the first few hours of a Saturday morning are the most enjoyable.

A few weeks ago, I was shuffling toward the garage with a steaming cup of coffee in one hand and the morning paper in the other. What began as a typical Saturday morning turned into one of those lessons that life seems to hand you from time to time. Let me tell you about it.

I turned the dial up into the phone portion of the band on my ham radio in order to listen to a Saturday morning swap net. Along the way, I came across an older sounding man, with a tremendous signal and a golden voice. You know the kind: he sounded like he should be in the broadcasting business. He was telling whomever he was talking with about "a thousand marbles." I was intrigued and stopped to listen to what he had to say.

"Well, Tom, it sure sounds like you're busy with your job. I'm sure they pay you well, but it's such a shame you have to be away from home and your family so much. Hard to believe a young fellow should have to work sixty or seventy hours a week to make ends meet. It is too bad you missed your daughter's dance recital." He continued. "Let me tell you something that has helped me keep my own priorities."

And that's when he began to explain his theory of a thousand marbles.

"You see, I sat down one day and did a little arithmetic. The average person lives about seventy-five years. I know, some live more and some live less, but on the average, folks live about seventy-five years

"Now then, I multiplied seventy-five times fifty-two, and I came up with 3,900, which is the number of Saturdays that the average person has in their entire lifetime. Now, stick with me, Tom, I'm getting to the important part.

"It took me until I was fifty-five years old to think about all of this in detail." He went on, "And by the time I had lived through over twenty-eight hundred Saturdays, I got to thinking that if I lived to be seventy-five, I only had about a thousand of them left to enjoy. So I went to a toy store and bought every single marble they had. I ended up having to visit three stores to round up one thousand marbles. I took them home and put them inside a large clear plastic container right here in the shack next to my gear.

"Every Saturday since then, I have taken one marble out and thrown it away. I found that by watching the marbles diminish, I focused more on the really important things in life. There is nothing like watching your time here on this earth run out to help get your priorities straight.

"Now let me tell you one last thing before I sign off with you and take my lovely wife out for breakfast. This morning, I took the very last marble out of the container. I figure that if I make it until next Saturday, then I have been given a little extra time. And the one thing we can all use is a little more time.

"It was nice to meet you, Tom, I hope you spend more time with your family, and I hope to meet you again here on the band. This is a seventy-five-year-old man, K9NZQ, clear and going QRT, good morning!"

You could have heard a pin drop on the band when this fellow signed off. I guess he gave us all a lot to think about. I had planned to work on the antenna that morning, and then I was going to meet up with a few hams to work on the next club newsletter.

Instead, I went upstairs and woke my wife up with a big kiss. "C'mon, honey, I'm taking you and the kids to breakfast."

"What brought this on?" she asked with a smile.

"Oh, nothing special, it's just been a long time since we spent a Saturday together with the kids. And hey, can we stop at a toy store while we are out? I need to buy some marbles."

A Sioux Indian Story

My grandfather took me to the fishing pond when I was about seven years-old and told me to throw a stone into the water. He told me to watch the circles created by the stone. Then he asked me to think of myself as that stone person.

"You may create lots of splashes in your life, but the waves that come from those splashes will disturb the peace of your fellow creatures," he said.

"Remember that you are responsible for what you put in your circle, and that circle will also touch many other circles."

"You will need to live in a way that allows the good that comes from your circle to send the peace of that goodness to others."

"The splash that comes from anger or jealousy will send those feelings to other circles. You are responsible for both."

That was the first time I realized each person creates the inner peace or discord that flows out into the world. We cannot create world peace if we are riddled with inner conflict, hatred, doubt, or anger. We radiate the feelings and thoughts that we hold inside, whether we speak them or not.

Whatever is splashing around inside of us is spilling out into the world, creating beauty or discord with all the other circles of life.

Remember the eternal wisdom: Whatever you focus on expands.

Mothers

Mothers think about our feelings.
Mothers think about our safety.
Mothers think about our health.
Mothers think we don't need all our toys.
Mothers think you should wash up every day.
Mothers think going to school is a good idea.
Mothers think you shouldn't eat too much candy.
Mothers think you should brush your teeth every day.
Mothers think of everything.

Mothers drive you lots of places, such as school, sports, and art classes.
Mothers help you with your homework.
Mothers keep us warm in winter.
Mothers serve great meals like lasagna, macaroni and cheese, and pizza.
Mothers keep our clothes clean and sew our buttons on.
Mothers keep us safe.
Mothers make delicious desserts like cookies, pies, and brownies.
Mothers work very hard. These are only a few of the things they do.

Mother say, "Don't wipe your hands on your pants."
Mothers say, "Don't forget to eat your breakfast."
Mothers say, "You're young, you'll get over it."
Mothers say, "Stop arguing with your brothers and sisters."
Mothers say, "Hurry up or you'll miss the bus."
Mothers say, "Don't sit so close to the TV."

Mothers say, "Clean your room."
Mothers say, "No elbows on the table."
Mothers say many important things they hope we remember.

Mothers are as warm as fresh baked muffins.
Mothers are like beautiful rainbows.
Mothers are like aspirin; they ease the pain.
Mothers are like Band-aids; they patch things up.
Mothers are as soft as a kitten's paw.
Mothers are like spring dew on a rose.
Mothers are like a cricket's music on a starlit night.
Mothers are as gentle as a puffy white cloud.
Mothers are as cool as a breeze in summer.
Mothers are like a blanket; they make us feel safe and warm.
Mothers are like nothing else in the world.

True Friendship

None of that sissy crap!

1. When you are sad—I will help you get drunk and plot revenge against the sorry bastard who made you sad.
2. When you are blue—I will try to dislodge whatever is choking you.
3. When you smile—I will know you finally got laid.
4. When you are scared—I will rag on you almost every chance I get.
5. When you are worried—I will tell you horrible stories about how much worse it could be until you quit whining.
6. When you are confused—I will use little words.
7. When you are sick—stay the hell away from me until you are well again. I do not want whatever you have.
8. When you fall—I will point and laugh at your clumsy ass.
9. This is my oath; I pledge it to the end. "Why?" you may ask. "Because you are my friend."
10. And always remember: when life hands you lemons, ask for tequila and salt and call me over!

About Being Old

The other day, a young person asked me how I felt about being old. I was taken aback, for I do not think of myself as old. Upon seeing my reaction, he was immediately embarrassed, but I explained that it was an interesting question, and I would ponder it and let him know.

Old age, I decided, is a gift!

I am now, probably for the first time in my life, the person I have always wanted to be. Oh, not my body! I sometimes despair over my body—the wrinkles, the baggy eyes, and the sagging bottom. And often, I am taken aback by that old person that lives in my mirror, but I do not agonize over those things for long.

I would never trade my amazing friends, my wonderful life, and my loving family for less gray hair or a flatter belly. As I've aged, I've become kinder to myself and less critical of myself.

I have become my own friend. I don't chide myself for eating that extra cookie, or for not making my bed, or for buying that silly cement gecko that I don't need but looks so *avant-garde* on my patio. I am entitled to overeat, to be messy, to be extravagant. I have seen too many dear friends leave this world too soon; before they understood the great freedom that comes with aging.

Whose business is it if I choose to read or play on the computer until 4:00 a.m. and sleep until noon? Or will dance with myself to those wonderful tunes of the '50s, and if I, at the same time, wish to weep over a lost love—I will!

I will walk the beach in a swimsuit that is stretched over a bulging body and will dive into the waves with abandon if I choose to, despite the pitying glances from the bikini set. They too will get old!

I know I am sometimes forgetful. But then again, some of life is just as well forgotten. And I eventually remember the important things. Sure, over the years my heart has been broken. How can your heart not break when you lose a loved one, or when a child suffers, or even when a beloved pet gets hit by a car?

But broken hearts give us strength, fortitude, understanding, and compassion. A heart never broken is pristine and sterile and will never know the joy of being imperfect. I am so blessed to have lived long enough to have my hair turn gray and skin toned, and to have my youthful laughs be forever etched into deep grooves on my face. So many have never laughed, and so many have died before their hair could turn silver. I can say, no and mean it. I can say, yes and mean it.

As you get older, it is easier to be positive. You care less about what other people think. I do not question myself anymore. I have earned the right to be wrong!

So to answer your question, I like being old. It has set me free. I like the person I have become. I am not going to live forever, but while I am here, I will not waste time lamenting what could have been or worrying about what will be.

And I shall eat dessert every single day.

The Kiss

A cabbie picks up a nun. She gets into the cab and notices that the *very* handsome cab driver won't stop staring at her. She asks him why he is staring.

He replies, "I have a question to ask, but I don't want to offend you."

She answers, "My son, you cannot offend me. When you have been a nun as long as I have, you get a chance to see and hear just about everything. I am sure there's nothing you could say or ask that I would find offensive."

"Well, I've always had a fantasy to have a nun kiss me."

She responds, "Well, let's see what we can do about that! You have to be single and you must be Catholic."

The cab driver is very excited and says, "Yes, I am single and Catholic!"

"Okay," the nun says. "Pull into the next alley."

The nun fulfills his fantasy with a kiss that would put most women to shame. But when they get back on the road, the cab driver starts feeling guilty.

"My dear child," said the nun, "why are you looking so sad?"

"Forgive me, but I have sinned. I lied, and I must confess. I am married, and I am Jewish."

The nun says, "Oh, that is okay. My name is Kevin, and I am going to a Halloween party!"

The Magic of Believing

by Edward J. McGrath Jr.
"An Exceptional View of Life"

I am not old enough to play baseball
Or football. I'm not eight yet.
My mom told me when you start baseball,
You aren't going to be able to run
That fast because you had an operation.

I told Mom I would not need to run
That fast. When I play baseball,
I'll just hit them out of the park.
Then I'll be able to walk

The Torch

Is there a magic cutoff period when offspring become accountable for their own actions? Is there a wonderful moment when parents can become detached spectators in the lives of their own children and shrug, "It's their life." And feel nothing?

When I was in my twenties, I stood in a hospital corridor, waiting for doctors to put a few stitches in my son's head. I asked, "When do you stop worrying?"

The nurse said, "When they get out of the accident stage."

My mother just smiled faintly and said nothing.

When I was in my thirties, I sat on a little chair in a classroom and heard how one of my children talked incessantly, disrupted the class, and was headed for a career of making license plates. As if to read my mind, a teacher said, "Don't worry, they all go through stages and then you can sit back, relax, and enjoy them."

My mother just smiled and said nothing.

When I was in my forties, I spent a lifetime waiting for the phone to ring, the cars to come home, the front door to open. A friend said, "They're trying to find themselves. Do not worry, in a few years, you can stop worrying. They will be adults."

My mother just smiled faintly and said nothing.

By the time I was fifty, I was sick and tired of being vulnerable. I was still worrying over my children, but there was a new wrinkle. There was nothing I could do about it.

My mother just smiled faintly and said nothing.

I continued to anguished over their failures, be tormented by their frustrations, and absorbed in their disappointments.

My friends said that when my kids got married, I could stop worrying and lead my own life. I wanted to believe them, but I was haunted by my mother's warm smile and her occasional, "You look pale, are you all right?" "Call me the minute you get home." "Drive carefully!"

Can it be that parents are sentenced to a lifetime of worry? Is concern for one another handed down like a torch to blaze the trail of human frailties and the fears of the unknown? Is concern a curse, or is it a virtue that elevates us to the highest form of life?

One of my children became quite irritable recently, saying to me, "Where are you? I've been calling for three days, and no one answered. I was worried."

I smiled a warm smile. The torch had been passed.

I Am the Flag of America

I am the flag of the United States of America.
My name is Old Glory.
I fly atop the world's tallest buildings.
I stand in watch in America's halls of justice.
I fly majestically over institutions of learning.
I stand guard with the power in the world.
Look up and see me.

I stand for peace, honor, truth, and justice.
I stand for freedom.
I am confident.
I am arrogant.
I am proud.
When I am flown with my fellow banners,
My head is a little higher,
My colors a little truer.

I bow to no one!
I am recognized all over the world.
I am worshipped—I am saluted.
I am loved—I am revered.
I am respected—and I am feared.

I have fought in every battle of every war for more than
Two hundred years.
I was flown at Valley Forge, Gettysburg, Shiloh, and Appomattox.
I was there at San Juan Hill, the trenches of France,

In the Argonne Forest, Anzio, Rome, and the beaches
Of Normandy.
Guam, Okinawa, Korea, and KheSan, Saigon, Vietnam knows me.

I am presently in the mountains of Afghanistan
And the hot dusty deserts of Iraq
And wherever freedom is needed.
I led my troops;
I was dirty, battleworn, and tired.
But my soldiers cheered me,
And I was proud.
I have been burned, torn, and trampled on the
Streets of countries I have helped set free.

I have been burned, soiled upon,
Burned, torn, and trampled in the streets of my country.
And when it is done by those whom I've served in battle—it hurts.

But I shall overcome—for I am strong.
I have slipped the bonds of Earth and stood watch
Over the unchartered frontiers of space from my vantage
Point on the moon.
I have borne silent witness to all of America's finest
Hours.
But my finest hours are yet to come.

When I am torn into strips and used as bandages
For my wounded comrades on the battlefield,
When I am flown at half-mast to honor my soldier,
Or when I lie in the trembling arms of a grieving parent
At the grave of their fallen son or daughter.

I Am Proud

A Son's Perspective

One day, the father of a very wealthy family took his son on a trip to the country with the express purpose of showing him how poor people live.

They spent a couple of days and nights on the farm of what would be considered a very poor family. On their return from the trip, the father asked the son, "How was the trip?"

"It was great, Dad."

"Did you see how poor people live?" the father asked.

"Oh yeah," said the son.

"So tell me, what did you learn from the trip?" asked the father.

The son answered, "I saw that we have one dog, and they have four. We have a pool that reaches to the middle of our garden, and they have a creek that has no end. We have imported lanterns in our garden, and they have the stars at night. Our patio reaches to the front yard, and they have a whole horizon. We have a small piece of land to live on, and they have fields that go beyond our sight. We have servants who serve us, but they serve others. We buy our food, they grow theirs. We have walls around our property to protect us, they have friends to protect them."

The boy's father was speechless.

Then his son added, "Thanks, Dad, for showing me how poor we are."

Isn't perspective a wonderful thing? Makes you wonder what would happen if we all gave thanks for everything we have, instead of worrying about what you do not have.

Appreciate every single thing you have, especially your friends and family!

The Airline Stewardess

While on a flight from New York, the stewardess was busy passing out peanuts and Cokes to everyone. There were about sixteen flights lined up waiting to take off. Then the other stewardess got a message from the pilot that the tower said the wind had changed 180 degrees, and they were the first in line to take off, and to have everyone buckle up. Without thinking, she just announced, "Please buckle up, grab your drinks, and hold your nuts, we're taking off!"

No one saw her for the rest of the flight to Houston, and all the other stewardesses were laughing all the way—and so were half of the passengers.

Walter Sondheim Jr.

An Obituary

A lifelong resident of Baltimore, Maryland, Sondheim was appointed to the city's school board in 1948. He didn't think much of local and state laws that required "separate but equal" segregated schools for whites and blacks.

By 1954, he was the board's president, and finally got his opening. The U.S. Supreme Court ordered schools to desegregate. Sondheim called all the board members and told them what he was going to do, and then the next day, he did it. "It was the first item to vote on, so I asked for discussion and then for the vote," he remembered later.

That vote made Baltimore's schools the first district south of the Mason-Dixon Line to desegregate, but the state school board president wasn't happy and tried to overturn the decision. He told the man "that he could come to Baltimore and try to unscramble the egg that we had scrambled if he wanted to," Sondheim recalled.

After the board's decision, a cross was burned on Sondheim's lawn, but "he would not back off," said former Maryland governor William Schaefer. "He would not step aside. He would not do anything except what was right. I've never known a man with so much integrity in my life."

Sondheim's impact on education, and Baltimore, did not end there. He led the redevelopment of the downtown area, and then chaired the governor's panel on school performance, which led the nation in demanding improvements in education, holding schools accountable for their performance.

In 1995, at the age of eighty-six, he was appointed to the state school board and, three years later, ended up as the board's president.

Mr. Sondheim died on February 15, 2007, in Baltimore from pneumonia. He was ninety-eight.

Brooklyn Tony on Ice Cream

(With a New York Accent)

The teacher asks her class, "If there a five birds sitting on a fence, and you shoot one of them, how many will be left?" She calls on Brooklyn Tony.

He replies, "None. They will fly away with the first gunshot."

The teacher replies, "The correct answer is four, but I like your thinking."

Then Brooklyn Tony says, "I have a question for you. There are three women sitting on a bench having ice cream. One is delicately licking the side of a triple scoop of ice cream. The second is gobbling down the top and sucking the cone. The third is biting off the top of the ice cream. Which one is married?"

The teacher, blushing a great deal, replied, "Well, I suppose the one that's gobbled down the top and sucked the cone."

To which Brooklyn Tony replied, "The correct answer is, 'the one with the wedding ring on. But I like your thinking."

Brooklyn Tony on Math

Brooklyn Tony returns from school and says he got an *F* in arithmetic.

"Why?" asks the father.

"The teacher asked, 'How much is two times three,' and I said six," replies Tony.

"But that's right!" says his dad.

"Yeah, but then she asked me, 'how much is three times two?'"

"What's the fucking difference?" asks the father.

That's what I said!

Brooklyn Tony on Grammar

Brooklyn Tony was sitting in class one day. All of a sudden, he needed to go to the bathroom. He yelled out, "Miss Jones, I need to take a piss!"

The teacher replied, "Now, Tony. That is not the proper word to use in this situation. The correct word you want to use is *urinate*. Please use the word *urinate* in a sentence correctly, and I will allow you to go."

Brooklyn Tony thinks for a bit, and then says, "You are an eight, but if you had bigger tits, you'd be a ten!"

Burglary in Florida

You Just Cannot Make This Stuff Up

When southern Florida resident Nathan Radlich's house was burglarized recently, thieves ignored his wide screen plasma TV, his VCR, and even left his Rolex watch. What they did take, however, was a generic white cardboard box filled with a grayish-white powder. (That's the way the police reported it.)

A spokesman for the Fort Lauderdale police said that it looked similar to high-grade cocaine, and they'd probably thought they'd hit the big time. Later, Nathan stood in front of numerous TV cameras and pleaded with the burglars, "Please return the cremated remains of my sister Gertrude. She died three years ago."

The next morning, the bullet-riddled corpse of a local drug dealer known as Hoochie Pevens was found on Nathan's doorstep. The cardboard box was there too, about half of Gertrude's ashes remained.

Scotched taped to the box was this note which said, "Hoochie sold us bogus blow, so we wasted Hoochie. Sorry we snorted your sister. No hard feelings. Have a nice day."

You Can... If You Think You Can

If you think you are beaten, then you are!
If you think you dare not, you don't
Success begins with your own will,
It is all in your state of mind.

Life's battles are not always won by those who are stronger and faster;
And sooner or later, the person who wins is the person who
Thinks he can!

Twenty-Five Signs That You Have Grown Up for Good

1. Your houseplants are alive, and you cannot smoke any of them.
2. Having sex in a twin bed is out of the question.
3. You keep more food than beer in the fridge.
4. Six o'clock in the morning is when you get up, not when you go to bed.
5. You hear your favorite song in the elevator.
6. You watch the weather channel.
7. Your friends marry and divorce instead of "hook up" and "break up."
8. You go from 130 days of vacation time to fourteen.
9. Jeans and a sweater no longer qualify as "dressed up."
10. You are the one calling the police because those $#%& kids next door will not turn their music down!
11. Older relatives feel comfortable telling sex jokes around you.
12. You do not know when Taco Bell closes anymore.
13. Your car insurance goes down, and your car payments go up.
14. You need to feed your dog the Science Diet instead of Mickey D's leftovers.
15. Sleeping on the couch makes your back hurt.
16. You take naps.
17. Dinner and a movie is the whole date instead of the beginning of one.

18. Eating a basket of chicken wings at 3:00 a.m. would severely upset, rather than settle, your stomach.
19. You go to the drug store for ibuprofen and antacid, not condoms and pregnancy tests.
20. A four-dollar bottle of wine is no longer "pretty good stuff."
21. You actually eat breakfast food at breakfast time.
22. "I just can't drink the way I used to" replaces "I'm never going to drink that much again."
23. Ninety percent of the time you spend in front of a computer is for real work.
24. You drink at home to save money before you go to the bar.
25. When you find out your friend is pregnant, you congratulate them instead of asking, "Oh nuts, what the hell happened?"

The Genius of Steven Wright

If you are not familiar with the work of Steven Wright, he's the famously erudite scientist and comic who once said, "I woke up one morning and all of my stuff had been stolen and replaced by exact duplicates."

1. I'd kill for a Nobel Peace Prize.
2. Borrow money from pessimists; they don't expect it back.
3. Half the people you know are below average.
4. Ninety-nine percent of lawyers give the rest a bad name.
5. 82.7 percent of all statistics are made up on the spot.
6. A conscience is what hurts when all your other parts feel so good.
7. A clear conscience is usually the sign of a bad memory.
8. If you want the rainbow, you got to put up with the rain.
9. Okay, what is the speed of dark?
10. I intend to live forever… so far, so good.
11. If Barbie is so popular, why do you have to buy her friends?
12. What happens if you get scared to death twice?
13. If at first you do not succeed, destroy all of the evidence.
14. Depression is merely anger without enthusiasm.
15. Why do psychics have to ask you for your name?
16. My mechanic told me, "I could not repair your brakes, so I made your horn louder."
17. "In conclusion" is the point where you get tired of thinking.
18. The problem with the gene pool is that there is no lifeguard.
19. To steal ideas from one person is plagiarism; to steal from many is research.

20. Everyone has a photographic memory; some just do not have any film.
21. The sooner you fall behind, the longer you'll have to catch up.

My New Car

I bought a new Lexus 350 and returned to the dealer the next day, complaining that I could not figure out how the radio worked.

The salesman explained that the radio was voice-activated. "Watch this" he said. "Nelson!"

The radio responded, "Ricky or Willie?"

"Willie," he continued. And "On the Road Again" came from the speakers.

Then he said, "Ray Charles!" And in an instant, "Georgia on My Mind" replaced Willie Nelson! I drove away happy, and for the next few days, every time I'd say, "Beethoven," I'd get beautiful classical music, and if I said, "Beatles," it gets one of their awesome songs.

Yesterday, a couple ran a red light and nearly creamed my new car, but I swerved in time to avoid them. I yelled, A——!" Immediately, the French National Anthem began to play, sung by Jane Fonda and Barbara Streisand, backed up by Michael Moore and the Dixie Chicks, with John Kerry on guitar, Al Gore on drums, Dan Rather on harmonica, Barbara Pelosi on tambourine, Harry Reid on spoons, Bill Clinton on sax, and Ted Kennedy on scotch.

Damn, I love that car.

A Three-Minute Management Course

Lesson 1

An eagle was sitting on a tree resting, doing nothing. A small rabbit saw the eagle and asked him, "Can I also sit like you and do nothing?"

The eagle answered, "Sure, why not!"

So the rabbit sat on the ground below the eagle and rested. All of a sudden, a fox appeared, jumped on the rabbit, and ate it.

Management Lesson

To be sitting and doing nothing, you must be sitting very, very high up.

Lesson 2

A turkey was chatting with a bull. "I would love to be able to get to the top of that tree," sighed the turkey, "but I haven't got the energy."

"Well, why don't you nibble on some of my droppings?" replied the bull. "They are packed with nutrients."

The turkey pecked at a lump of dung, and found it actually gave him strength to reach the lowest branch; and, finally, after a fortnight, the turkey was proudly perched at the top of the tree. He was promptly spotted by a farmer who shot him out of the tree.

Management Lesson

Bullshit might get you to the top, but it won't keep you there.

Lesson 3

A little bird was flying south for the winter. It was so cold, the bird froze and fell to the ground into a large field; then a cow came by and dropped some dung on him. As the frozen bird lay there in the pile of cow dung, he began to realize how warm it was. The dung was actually thawing him out! He laid there all warm and happy and soon began to sing for joy.

A passing cat heard the bird singing and came to investigate. Following the sound, the cat discovered the bird under the pile of cow dung and promptly ate him.

Management Lesson

1. Not everyone who shits on you is your enemy.
2. Not everyone who gets you out of shit is your friend.
3. And when you are in deep shit, it is best to keep your mouth shut.

This seminar in management is adjourned!

Psychological Christmas Carols

Schizophrenia: Do You Hear What I Hear?

Multiple personality disorder: We Three Kings Disorientated Are

Dementia: I Think I'll be Home for Christmas

Narcissistic: Hark the Herald Angels Sing About Me

Manic: Deck the Halls and Walls and House and Lawn and Streets and Stores and Office and Town and Cars and Busses and Trucks and Trees

Paranoid: Santa Claus Is Coming to Town to Get Me

Personality disorder: You Better Watch Out, I'm Gonna Cry, I'm Gonna Pout, Maybe I'll Tell You Why!

Attention deficit disorder: Silent night, Holy—ooh look at the Froggy—can I have a chocolate, why is France so far away?

Obsessive-compulsive disorder—Jingle Bells, Jingle Bells, Jingle Bells, Jingle Bells, Jingle Bells, Jingle Bells, Jingle Bells, Jingle Bells, Jingle Bells, Jingle Bells, Jingle Bells, Jingle Bells, Jingle Bells, Jingle Bells, Jingle Bells, Jingle Bells, Jingle Bells. Jingle Bells, Jingle Bells, Jingle Bells, Jingle Bells, Jingle Bells, Jingle Bells, Jingle Bells, Jingle Bells, Jingle Bells, Jingle Bells, Jingle Bells, Jingle Bells, Jingle Bells, Jingle Bells, Jingle Bells, Jingle Bells, Jingle Bells.

Long Ago and Far Away

In a land that time forgot,
Before the days of Dylan
Or the dawn of Camelot.
There lived a race of innocents,
And they were you and me,
Long ago and far away
In the land of Sandra Dee.

Oh, there was truth and goodness
In that land where we were born,
Where navels were for oranges,
And Peyton Place was porn.
For Ike was in the White House,
And Hoss was on TV.
And God was in heaven
In the land of Sandra Dee.

We learned to gut a muffler,
We washed our hair at dawn,
We spread our crinolines to dry
In circles on the lawn.
And they could hear us coming
All the way to Tennessee,
All starched and sprayed and rumbling
In the land of Sandra Dee.

We longed for love and romance,
And waited for the prince,
And Eddie Fisher married Liz,
And no one's seen him since.
We danced to "Little Darlin'"
And sang to "Stagger Lee"
And cried for Buddy Holly
In the land of Sandra Dee.

Only girls wore earrings then,
And three was one too many,
And only boys wore flat-top cuts,
Except for Jean McKinney.
And only in our wildest dreams
Did we expect to see
A boy named George in Lipstick
In the land of Sandra Dee.

We fell for Frankie Avalon,
Annette was oh, so nice,
And when they made a movie,
They never made it twice.
We did not have a Star Trek Five,
Or Psycho Two and Three,
Or Rocky-Rambo Twenty
In the land of Sandra Dee.

Miss Kitty had a heart of gold,
And Chester had a limp,
And Reagan was a Democrat
Whose co-star was a chimp.
We had a Mr. Wizard,
But not a Mr. T,
And Oprah could not talk yet
In the land of Sandra Dee.

We had our share of heroes,
We never thought they would go,
At least not Bobby Darin,
Or Marilyn Monroe.
For youth was still eternal,
And life was yet to be,
And Elvis was forever,
In the land of Sandra Dee.

We had never heard the rock band
That was Grateful to be Dead,
And Airplanes weren't named Jefferson,
And Zeppelins were not Led.
And Beatles lives in gardens then,
And Monkees in a tree,
Madonna was a virgin
In the land of Sandra Dee.

We had never heard of microwaves,
Or telephones in cars,
And babies might be bottle fed,
But they were not grown in jars.
And "gay" meant fancy-free,
And dorms were never coed
In the land of Sandra Dee.

We had not seen enough of jets
To talk about lag,
And microchips were what was left,
At the bottom of the bag.
And hardware was a box of nails,
And bytes came from a flea,
And rocket ships were fiction
In the land of Sandra Dee.

Buicks came with portholes,
And side shows came with freaks,
And bathing suits came big enough
To cover both your cheeks.
And Coke came just in bottles,
And skirts came to the knee,
And Castro came into power
In the land of Sandra Dee.

We had no Crest with fluoride,
We had no Hill Street Blues,
We all wore superstructure bras
Designed by Howard Hughes.
We had no patterned pantyhose
Or Lipton herbal tea
Or prime-time ads for condoms
In the land of Sandra Dee.

There were no golden arches,
No Perrier's to chill,
And fish were not called Wanda,
And cats were not called Bill.
And middle-aged was thirty-five
And old was forty-three,
And ancient were our parents
In the land of Sandra Dee.

But all things have a season,
Or so we have heard them say,
And now instead of Maybelline
And they send us invitations
To join AARP,
We have come a long way, baby,
In the land of Sandra Dee.

So now we face a brave new world,
In slightly larger jeans,
And wonder why they're using
Smaller print in magazines.
And we tell our children's children
Of the way it used to be,
Long, long ago and far away
In the land of Sandra Dee.

A Letter to Dad

A father passing by his son's bedroom was astonished to see that his bed was nicely made and everything was picked up. Then he saw an envelope propped up prominently on the pillow that was addressed to "Dad." With the worst premonition, he opened the envelope with trembling hands and read the letter.

Dear Dad,

It is with great regret and sorrow that I am writing to you. I had to elope with my new girlfriend because I wanted to avoid a scene with Mom and you. I have been finding real passion with Stacy, and she is so nice.

I knew you might not approve of her because of all her piercings, tattoos, tight motorcycle clothes, and the fact that she is much older than I am—twenty. But it is not just the passion… Dad, she is pregnant.

Stacy said that we will be very happy. She owns a trailer in the woods and has a stack of firewood for the whole winter. We share a dream of having many more children. Stacy has opened my eyes to the fact that marijuana does not really hurt anyone. We will be growing it for ourselves and trading with other people that live nearby for cocaine and ecstasy.

In the meantime, we will pray that science will find a cure for AIDS so Stacy can get better. She deserves it. Do not worry, Dad. I am fifteen, and I know how to take care of myself. Someday, I am sure we will be back to visit so that you can get to know your grandchildren.

Love,
Your son, John

PS: Dad, none of the above is true. I am over at Tommy's house. I just wanted to remind you that there are worse things in life than the report card that is in my center drawer. I love you. Call me when it is safe to come home.

The Gingham Dress

A True Story by Malcolm Forbes

A lady in a faded gingham dress and her husband dressed in a home-spun threadbare suit, stepped off the train in Boston, and walked timidly without an appointment into the Harvard University president's outer office.

The secretary could tell in a moment that such backwoods, country hicks had no business at Harvard and probably did not even deserve to be in Cambridge.

"We'd like to see the president," the man softly said.

"He will be busy all day," the secretary snapped.

"We'll wait," the lady replied.

For hours, the secretary ignored them, hoping that the couple would finally become discouraged and go away. They did not, and the secretary grew frustrated and finally decided to disturb the president, even though it was a chore she always regretted.

"Maybe if you see them for a few minutes, they will leave," she said to him.

He sighed in exasperation and nodded. Someone of this importance obviously did not have the time to spend with them, and he detested gingham dresses and homespun suits cluttering up his outer office.

The president, stern-faced and with dignity, strutted toward the couple.

The lady told him, "We had a son who attended Harvard for one year. He loved Harvard. He was happy here. But about a year ago, he was accidentally killed. My husband and I would like to erect a memorial to him, somewhere on campus."

The president was not touched. He was shocked.

"Madam," he said gruffly, "we can't put up a statue for every person who attended Harvard and dies. If we did, this place would look like a cemetery."

"Oh no," the lady explained quickly. "We do not want Harvard to erect a statue. We thought we would like to give a building to Harvard."

The president rolled his eyes. He glanced at the gingham dress and homespun suit, and then exclaimed, "A building! Do you have any earthly idea how much a building costs? We have over seven and a half million dollars in the physical buildings here at Harvard."

For a moment, the lady was silent. The president was pleased. Maybe he could get rid of them now. The lady turned to her husband and said quietly, "Is that all it cost to start a university? Why don't we start our own?"

Her husband nodded. The president's face wilted in confusion and bewilderment.

Mr. and Mrs. Leland Stanford got up and walked away, traveling to Palo Alto, California, where they established the university that bears their name, Stanford University, a memorial to a son that Harvard no longer cared about.

You can easily judge the character of others by how they treat those who they think can do nothing for them.

Congratulations to all the kids who were born in the 1940s, 1950s, 1960s, and 1970s!

First, we survived being born to mothers who smoked and/or drank while they carried us. They took aspirin, ate blue cheese dressing, tuna from a tin, and didn't get tested for diabetes. Then after that trauma, our baby cots were covered with bright colored lead-based paints. We had no childproof lids on medicine bottle, doors, or cabinets—and when we rode ours bikes, we had no helmets, not to mention the risks we took hitchhiking.

As children, we would ride in cars with no seatbelts or air bags. Riding in the back of a van was always great fun. We drank water from the garden hosepipe and *not* from a bottle. We shared one soft drink with four friends, from one bottle, and no one actually died from this. We ate cakes, white bread, and real butter and drank pop with sugar in it, but we weren't overweight because we were always playing outside.

We would leave home in the morning and play ball all day, as long as we were back when the streetlights came on. No one was able to reach us all day. And we were okay.

We would spend hours building our go-carts out of scraps and then ride down the hill, only to find out we forgot the brakes. After running into the bushes a few times, we learned to solve the problem.

We did not have Playstations, Nintendos, Xboxes—no video games at all—no ninety-nine channels on cable, no video tape movies, no surround sound, no cell phones, no text messaging, no personal computers, no Internet chat rooms. We had friends, and we went outside and found them.

We fell out of trees, got cut, broke bones and teeth, and there were no lawsuits from these accidents. We played with worms and mud pies made from dirt, and the worms did not live in us forever. We made up games with sticks and tennis balls, and although we were told it would happen, we did not poke out any eyes.

We rode bikes or walked to a friend's house and knocked on the door or rang the bell, or just yelled for them. Local teams had tryouts, and not everyone made the team. Those who did not had to learn to deal with disappointment. Imagine that!

The idea of a parent bailing us out if we broke the law was unheard of. They actually sided with the law!

This generation has produced some of the best risk-takers, problem-solvers, and inventors ever. The past fifty years have been an explosion of innovation and new ideas.

We had freedom, failure, success, and responsibility—and we learned *how to deal with it all!*

If you are one of them, congratulations!

You might want to share this with others who have grown up as kids before the lawyers and government regulated our lives for our own good.

And while you are at it, make a copy of this item and send it to your children so they will know how brave their parents were.

Kind of makes you want to run through the house with scissors, doesn't it?

The Hospital Window

A great note for all to read. It will take thirty-seven seconds to read this and change your thinking forever.

Two men, both seriously ill, occupied the same hospital room. One man was allowed to sit up in his bed for an hour each afternoon to help drain the fluid from his lungs. His bed was next to the room's only window. The other man had to spend all of his time flat on his back. The men talked for hours on end. They spoke of their wives and families, their homes, their jobs, their involvement in the military service, where they had been on vacations.

Every afternoon, when the man in the bed by the window could sit up, he would pass the time by describing to his roommate all the things he could see outside the window.

The man in the other bed began to live for those one-hour periods where his world would be broadened and enlivened by all the activity and color of the world outside.

The window overlooked a park with a lovely lake. Ducks and swans played on the water while children sailed model boats. Young lovers walked arm-in-arm amidst flowers of every color, and a fine view of the city skyline could be seen in the distance.

As the man by the window described all this in exquisite detail, the man on the other side of the room would close his eyes and imagine the picturesque scene. One warm afternoon, the man by the window described a parade passing by. Although the other man could not hear the band, he could see it in his mind's eye as the gentleman by the window portrayed it with descriptive words.

Days and weeks passed. One morning, the nurse arrived to bring water for their baths only to find the lifeless body of the man by the window, who had died peacefully in his sleep. She was saddened and called the hospital attendants to take the body away.

As soon as it seemed appropriate, the other man asked if he could be moved next to the window. The nurse was happy to make the switch, and after making sure he was comfortable, she left him alone. Slowly, painfully, he propped himself up on one elbow to take his first look at the real world outside.

He strained to slowly turn to look out the window beside the bed. It faced a blank wall.

The man asked the nurse what could have compelled his deceased roommate who had described such wonderful things outside this window. The nurse responded that the man was blind and could not see the wall. She said, "Perhaps he just wanted to encourage you."

Epilogue

There is tremendous happiness in making others happy, despite our own situations. Shared grief is half the sorrow, but happiness, when shared, is doubled.

If you want to feel rich, just count all the things you have that money can't buy. "Today is a gift, that is why it is called the present."

Too Busy for a Friend

One day, a teacher asked her students to list the names of the other students in the room on two sheets of paper, leaving a space between each name. Then she told them to think of the nicest thing they could say about each of their classmates and write it down.

It took the remainder of the class period to finish their assignment, and as the students left the room, each one handed in the papers.

That Saturday, the teacher wrote down the name of each student on a separate sheet of paper and listed what everyone had said about that individual.

On Monday, she gave each student his or her list. Before long, the entire class was smiling. "Really?" she heard whispered. "I never knew that I meant anything to anyone!" And "I didn't know others liked me so much" were most of the comments.

No one ever mentioned those papers in class again. She never knew if they discussed them after class or with their parents, but it didn't matter. The exercise had accomplished its purpose. The students were happy with themselves and one another. That group of students moved on.

Several years later, one of the students was killed in Vietnam, and his teacher attended the funeral of that special student. She had never seen a serviceman in a military coffin before. He looked so handsome and so mature.

The church was packed with his friends. One by one, those who loved him took a last walk by the coffin. The teacher was the last one to bless the coffin.

As she stopped there, one of the soldiers who acted as a pallbearer came up to her. "Were you Mark's math teacher?" he asked.

She nodded yes.

Then he said, "Mark talked about you a lot."

After the funeral, most of Mark's former classmates went together to a luncheon. Mark's mother and father were there, obviously waiting to speak with his teacher.

"We want to show you something." His father said, taking a wallet out of his pocket. "They found this on Mark when he was killed. We thought you might recognize it."

Opening the billfold, he carefully removed two worn pieces of notebook paper that had obviously been taped, folded, and refolded many times. The teacher knew without looking that the papers were the ones on which she had listed all the good things each of Mark's classmates had said about him.

"Thank you so much for doing that," Mark's mother said. "As you can see, Mark treasured it."

All of Mark's former classmates started to gather around. Charlie smiled rather sheepishly and said, "I still have my list. It is in the top drawer of my desk at home."

Chuck's wife said, "Chuck has asked me to place it in our wedding album."

"I have mine too," Marilyn said. "It's in my diary."

Then Vicki, another classmate, reached into her pocketbook, took out her wallet, and showed her worn and frazzled list to the group. "I carry this with me at all times," Vicki said, and without batting an eyelash, she continued, "I think we all saved our lists."

That is when the teacher finally sat down and cried. She cried for Mark and all of his friends who would never see him again.

The density of people in society is so thick that we forget that life will end one day. And we do not know when that one day will be.

So please, tell the people you love and care for that they are special and important. Tell them now before it is too late.

Dedicated to Mike Cartwright

The Gunslinger and the Old Prospector

An old prospector walks his tired old mule into a Western town one day. He'd been out in the desert for about six months without a drop of whiskey. He walked up to the first saloon he came to and tied his old mule to the hitching rail.

As he stood there brushing some of the dust from his face and clothes, a gunslinger walked out of the saloon with a gun in one hand and a bottle of whiskey in the other.

The gunslinger looked at the old man and laughed, saying, "Hey old man, have you ever danced?"

The old man looked up at the gunslinger and said, "No, I never did dance, I just never wanted to."

A crowd had gathered by then, and the gunslinger said, "Well, you old fool, you're going to dance now, and started shooting at the old man's feet."

The old prospector was hopping around, and everybody was laughing.

When the gunslinger fired his last bullet, he holstered his gun and turned around to go back into the saloon.

The old man reached up on his mule, drew his shotgun, and pulled bother hammers back making double clicking sound.

The gunslinger heard the sound and everything got quiet. The crowd watched the gunslinger slowly turn around looking down bother barrels of the shotgun.

The old man asked, "Did you ever kiss a mule square on the ass?"

The gunslinger swallowed hard and said, "No, but I've always wanted to."

The morale of the story: Don't mess with old farts.

The Frog

A man takes the day off from work and decides to go out golfing. He is on the second hole when he notices a frog sitting next to the green. He thinks nothing of it and is about to shoot when he hears, "Ribbit 9 Iron."

The man looks around and doesn't see anyone. Again, he hears, "Ribbit 9 Iron." He looks at the frog and decides to prove the frog wrong, puts the club away, and grabs a 9 Iron.

Boom!

He hits it ten inches from the cup. He is shocked. He says to the frog, "Wow that is amazing. You must be a lucky frog."

The frog replies, "Ribbit lucky frog."

The man decides to take the frog with him to the next hole.

"What do you think, frog?" the man asks.

"Ribbit 3 wood."

The guy takes out 3 Wood and *boom!* A hole in one. The man is befuddled and doesn't know what to say. By the end of the day, the man golfed the best game of golf in his life and asks the frog, "Okay, where to next?"

The frog replies, "Ribbit, Las Vegas."

They go to Vegas and the guy says, "Okay, frog, now what?"

The frog says, "Ribbit, roulette."

Upon approaching the roulette table, the man asks, "What do you think I should be?"

The frog replies, "Ribbit $3000, black 6."

Now, this is a one-in-a-million shot to win, but after the golf game, the man figures what the heck. *Boom!* Tons of cash comes sliding back across the table.

The man takes his winnings and buys the best room in the hotel. He sits down with the frog at his feet and says, "Frog, I do not know what to do with all of this money, and I am forever grateful."

The frog replies, "Ribbit, kiss me."

He figures why not, since after all the frog did for him, he deserves it. With a kiss, the frog turns into a gorgeous fifteen-year-old girl.

"And that, Your Honor, is how the girls ended up in my room. So help me God, or my name is not William Jefferson Clinton."

What Teachers Make

The dinner guests were sitting around the table, discussing life.

One man, a CEO, decided to explain the problem with education. He argued, "What's a kid going to learn from someone who decided his best option in life was to become a teacher?" He reminded the other dinner guests what they say about teachers: "Those who can, do. Those who can't, teach."

To stress his point, he said to another guest, "You are a teacher, Bonnie. Be honest. What do you make?"

Bonnie, who had a reputation for honesty and frankness replied, "You want to know what I make?" She paused for a second, then began. "Well, I make kids work harder than they ever thought they could. I make a C+ feel like the Congressional Medal of Honor. I make kids sit through forty minutes of class time when their parents can't make them sit for five without an iPod, Game Cube, or movie rental."

"You want to know what I make?" She paused again and looked at each and every person at the table.

"I make kids wonder. I make them question. I make them criticize. I make them apologize and mean it. I make them have respect and take responsibility for their actions. I teach them to write and then I make them write. I make them read, read, read. I make them show all their work—in math. I make my students from other countries learn everything they need to know in English while preserving their unique cultural identity. I make my classroom a place where all my students feel safe. I make my students stand to say the Pledge of Allegiance to the Flag because we live in the United States of America. Finally, I make them understand that if they use all the gifts they were given, work hard, and follow their hearts, they can succeed in life."

Bonnie paused one last time, and then continued, "Then, when people try to judge me by what I make, I can hold my head up high and pay no attention because they are ignorant. You want to know what I make? I make a *difference*. What do you make?"

I Believe

I believe that we do not have to change friends if we understand that friends change.

I believe that no matter how good a friend is, they are going to hurt you every once in a while, and you must forgive them for that.

I believe that true friendship continues to grow, even over the longest distance. Same goes for true love.

I believe that you can do something in an instant that will give you heartache for a lifetime.

I believe that it is taking me a long time to become the person I want to be.

I believe that you should always leave loved ones with loving words. It may be the last time you see them.

I believe that you can keep going long after you can't.

I believe that we are responsible for what we do, no matter how we feel.

I believe that either you control your attitude, or it controls you.

I believe in the Boston Red Sox, the Boston Celtics, the Boston Bruins, and the New England Patriots.

I believe that regardless of how hot and steamy a relationship is at first, the passion fades, and there had better be something else to take its place.

I believe that heroes are ordinary people who did what had to be done when it needed to be done, regardless of the consequences.

I believe that money is a lousy way of keeping score.

I believe that my best friend and I can do anything or nothing and have the best time!

I believe that sometimes the people you expect to kick you when you are down will be the ones to help you get back up.

I believe that sometimes when I am angry, I have the right to be angry—but that does not give me the right to be cruel.

I believe that just because someone does not love you the way you want them to, it does not mean they do not love you with all they have.

I believe that maturity has more to do with what types of experiences you have had and what you have learned from them and less to do with how many birthdays you have celebrated.

I believe that it is not always enough to be forgiven by other. Sometimes you have to learn to forgive yourself.

I believe that no matter how bad your heart is broken, the world does not stop for your grief.

I believe that our background and circumstances may have influenced who we are but are not responsible for who we become.

I believe that just because two people argue, it does not mean they do not love each other; and just because they do not argue, it does not mean they do.

I believe you should not be eager to find out a secret. It could change your life forever.

I believe that two people can look at the same thing and see something totally different.

I believe that your life can change in a matter of hours by people who do not even know you.

I believe that even when you think you have no more to give, when a friend cries out to you—you will find the strength to help.

I believe the credentials on the wall do not make you a decent human being.

I believe that the people you care about most in life are taken from you too soon.

The Pledge of Allegiance

by Senator John McCain

As you may know, I spent five and one half years as a prisoner of war during the Vietnam War. In the early years of our imprisonment, the NVA kept us in solitary confinement or two or three to a cell. In 1971, the NVA moved us from these conditions of isolation into large rooms with as many as thirty or forty men to a room.

This was, as you can imagine, a wonderful change and was a direct result of the efforts of millions of Americans on behalf of a few hundred POWs ten thousand miles from home. One of the men who moved into my room was a young man named Mike Christian.

Mike came from a small town near Selma, Alabama. He did not wear a pair of shoes until he was thirteen years old. At seventeen, he enlisted in the United States Navy. He later earned a commission by going to Officer's Training School. Then he became a naval flight officer and was shot down and captured in 1967. Mike had a keen and deep appreciation of the opportunities this country and our military provide for people who want to work and want to succeed.

As part of the change in treatment, the Vietnamese allowed some prisoners to receive packages from home. In some of these packages, there were handkerchiefs, scarves, and other items of clothing. Mike got himself a bamboo needle. Over a period of a couple of months, he created and American flag and sewed it on the inside of his shirt. Every afternoon, before we had a bowl of soup, we would hang Mike's shirt on the wall of the cell and say the Pledge of Allegiance.

I know the Pledge of Allegiance may not seen the most import-ant part of our day now, but I can assure you that in that stark cell, it was indeed the most important and meaningful event. One day, the Vietnamese searched our cell, as they did periodically, and discovered Mike's shirt with the flag sewn inside and removed it.

That evening, they returned, opened the door of the cell, and for the benefit of all of us, beat Mike Christian severely for the next couple of hours. Then, they opened the door of the cell and threw him in. We cleaned him up as well as we could.

The cell in which we lived had a concrete slab in the middle on which we slept. Four naked light bulbs hung in each corner of the room.

As I said, we tried to clean up Mike as well as we could. After the excitement died down, I looked in the corner of the room, and sitting there beneath that dim light bulb with a piece of red cloth, another shirt, and his bamboo needle was my friend Mike Christian. He was sitting there with his eyes almost shut from the beating he had received, making another American flag. He was not making the flag because it made him feel better. He was making the flag because he knew how important it was to us to be able to pledge allegiance to our flag and country.

So the next time you say the Pledge of Allegiance, you must never forget the sacrifice and courage that thousands of Americans have made to build our nation and promote freedom around the world. You must remember our duty, our honor, and our country.

"I pledge allegiance to flag of the United States of America and to the republic for which it stands, one nation under God, indivisible, with liberty and justice for all."

The School Answering Machine

This is an actual answering machine message for the school. This came about because they implemented a policy of requiring students and parents to be responsible for their children's absences and missing homework.

The school and teachers are being sued by parents who want their children's failing grades changed to passing grades, even though these children were absent fifteen to thirty times during the semester and did not complete enough schoolwork to pass their classes.

The outgoing message: "Hello! You have reached the automated answering service of our high school. In order to assist you in connecting to the right staff member, please listen to all the options before making a selection. To lie about why your child is out, press 1; to make excuses for why your child did not do his work, press 2; to complain about what we do, press 3; to swear at staff members, press 4; to ask why you did not get information that was already enclosed in your newsletter and several flyers mailed to you, press 5; if you want us to raise your child, press 6; if you want to reach out and touch, slap, or hit someone, press 7; to request another teacher for the third time this year, press 8; to complain about bus transportation, press 9;   to complain about school lunches, press 0.

"If you realize this is the real world and your child must be accountable and responsible for his/her own behavior, class work, homework, and that it's not the teachers' fault for your child's lack of effort, hang up and have a nice day! If you want this in Spanish, you must be in the wrong country."

A Special Phone Call

John Madden, a sports announcer, was in Buffalo to announce a football game one weekend when he noticed a special telephone near the Bills bench. He asked Drew Bledsoe what it was used for and was told it was a hotline to God. John asked if he could use it. Drew told him, "Sure, but it will cost you two hundred dollars." John scratched his head, then thought, *What the heck, I could use some help in picking games this week*. He pulled out his wallet and paid two hundred dollars.

John's picks were perfect for the week.

The next week, John was in Indianapolis when he noticed the same kind of phone on the Colts bench. He asked what the telephone was for, and Peyton Manning told him, "It's a hotline to God. If you want to use it, it will cost you five hundred dollars." Recalling last week, John pulled out his wallet and made the call.

John's picks were perfect again that week.

The next weekend, John was in Foxboro at Gillette Stadium when he noticed the same kind of telephone by the Patriots bench. He asked Tom Brady, "Is that the hotline to God?"

Tom replied, "Yes, and if you want to use it, it will cost you thirty-five cents."

John looked incredulously at Brady and said, "Wait a second, I just paid $200 in Buffalo and $500 in Indianapolis to use the same phone to God! Why do the Patriots only charge thirty-five cents?"

Tom Brady looked at John Madden and replied, "Because in New England, it's a local call."

The Pickle Jar

The pickle jar, as far back as I can remember, sat on the floor beside the dresser in my parents' bedroom. When he got ready for bed, Dad would empty his pockets and toss the coins into the jar.

As a small boy, I was always fascinated at the sounds the coins made as they were dropped into the jar. They landed with a merry jingle when the jar was almost empty. Then the tones gradually muted to a dull thud as the jar was filled.

I used to squat on the floor in front of the jar and admire the copper and silver circles that glinted like a pirate's treasure when the sun poured through the bedroom window. When the jar was filled, Dad would sit at the kitchen table and roll the coins before taking them to the bank. Taking the coins to the bank was always a big production. Stacked neatly in a small cardboard box, the coins were placed between Dad and me on the seat of his old truck.

Each time, as we drove to the bank, Dad would look at me hopefully. "Those coins are going to keep you out of the textile mill, son. You're going to do better than me. This old mill town's not going to hold you back."

Also, each and every time, as he slid the box of rolled coins across the counter at the bank toward the cashier, he would grin proudly and say, "These are for my son's college fund. He'll never work at the mill all his life like me." He would always celebrate each deposit by stopping for an ice cream cone. I always got chocolate, and Dad would always got vanilla. When the clerk at the ice cream parlor handed Dad his change, he would show me the few coins nestled in his palm and say, "When we get home, we'll start filling the jar again." He always let me drop the first coins into the empty jar. As they rattled around with a brief, happy jingle, we grinned at each other. "You'll get to college on pennies, nickels, dimes, and quarters," he said. "But you'll get there. I'll see to that."

The years passed, and I finished college and took a job in another town. Once, while visiting my parents, I used the phone in their bedroom and noticed that the pickle jar was gone. It served its purpose and had been removed.

A lump rose in my throat as I stared at the spot beside the dresser where the jar had always stood. My dad was a man of few words and never lectured me on the values of determination, perseverance, and faith. The pickle jar had taught me all these virtues far more eloquently than the most flowery word could have done.

When I married, I told my wife Susan about the significant part the lowly pickle jar had played in my life as a boy. In my mind, it defined more than anything else how much my dad had loved me. No matter how rough things got at home, Dad continued to doggedly drop his coins into the jar. Even the summer when Dad got laid off from the mill and Mama had to serve dried beans several times a week, not a single dime was taken from the jar.

To the contrary, as Dad looked across the table at me, pouring catsup over my beans to make them palatable, he became more determined than ever to make a way out for me. "When you finish college, son," he told me, his eyes glistening, "you'll never have to eat beans again—unless you want to."

The first Christmas after our daughter Jessica was born, we spent the holiday with my parents. After dinner, Mom and Dad sat next to each other on the sofa, taking turns cuddling their first grandchild. Jessica began to whimper softly, and Susan took her from Dad's arms. "She probably needs to be changed," she said, carrying the baby into my parents' bedroom to diaper her. When Susan came back into the living room, there was a strange mist in her eyes.

She handed Jessica back to Dad before taking my hand and leading me into the room. "Look," she said softly, her eyes directing me to a spot on the floor beside the dresser. To my amazement, there, as if it had never been removed, stood the old pickle jar with some coins in it. I walked over to the pickle jar, dug down into my pocket, and pulled out a fistful of coins. With a gamut of emotions chocking me, I dropped the coins into the jar. I looked up and saw Dad, carrying Jessica, had slipped quietly into the room. Our eyes locked, and I knew he was feeling the same emotions I felt. Neither one of us could speak.

Stories like this one truly touch your heart as it has mine. Sometimes we are too busy adding up our troubles that we forget to count our blessings.

Never underestimate the power of your actions. With one small gesture, you can change a person's life for better or for worse.

Why, Why, Why?

Why do we press harder on the remote control when we know the batteries are going dead?

Why do banks charge a fee on "insufficient funds" when they know there is not enough money?

Why does someone believe you when you say there are four billion stars, but check when you say the paint is wet?

Why does glue stick to the bottle?

Why do they use sterilized needles for death by lethal injection?

Why does Superman duck when a criminal throws a gun at him?

Why doesn't Tarzan have a beard?

Why does Superman stop bullets with his chest, but ducks when you throw a revolver at him?

Why do kamikaze pilots wear helmets?

If people evolved from apes, why are there still apes?

Why is it that no matter what color bubble bath you use, the bubbles are always white?

Is there ever a day that mattresses are not on sale?

Why do people constantly return to the refrigerator with hopes that something new to eat will have materialized?

Why do people run over a piece of string a dozen times with their vacuum cleaner and then reach down, pick it up, examine it, then put it down to give the vacuum one more chance?

Why is it that no plastic bag will open from the end on the first try?

How do those dead bugs get into those enclosed light fixtures?

How come you never hear father-in-law jokes?

In winter, why do we try to keep the house as warm as it was in the summer when we complained about the heat?

The statistics on sanity are that one in four persons is suffering from some sort of mental illness. Then think of your three best friends. If they are okay, then it's you!

Amen to the Words of Paul Harvey

Paul Harvey says...

I do not believe in Santa Claus, but I'm not going to sue somebody for singing a ho-ho-ho song in December. I do not agree with Darwin, but I did not go out and hire a lawyer when my high school teacher taught the theory of evolution.

Life, liberty, or your pursuit of happiness will not be endangered because someone says a thirty-second prayer before a football game.

So what is the big deal? It is not like somebody is up there reading the entire book of Acts. They're just talking to a god they believe in and asking him to grant safety to the players on the field and the fans going home from the game.

But it is a Christian prayer, some will argue.

Yes, and this is the United States of America, a country founded on Christian principles. According to our own phone book, Christian churches outnumber all others better than two hundred to one. So what would you expect? Someone chanting in Hare Krishna?

If I went to a football game in Jerusalem, I would expect to hear a Jewish prayer. If I went to Baghdad, I would expect to hear a Muslim prayer. If I went to a ping-pong match in China, I would expect to hear someone pray to Buddha. And I would not be offended. It would not bother me one bit. *When in Rome.*

But what about the atheists? Is this another argument? What about them? Nobody is asking them to be baptized. We are not going to pass the collection plate. Just humor us for thirty seconds. If that is asking too much, bring a Walkman or a pair of earplugs. Go to the bathroom. Visit the concession stand. Call your lawyer!

Unfortunately, one or two will make that call. One or two will tell thousands what they can and cannot do. I do not think a short prayer at a football game is going to shake the world's foundation.

Christians are just sick and tired of turning the other cheek while our courts strip us of all our rights. Our parents and grandparents taught us to pray before eating, to pray before we go to sleep. Our Bible tells us to pray without ceasing. Now a handful of people and their lawyers are telling us to cease praying.

God help us! And if that last sentence offends you, well just sue me!

The Spanish Lesson

A Spanish teacher was explaining to her class that in Spanish, unlike English, nouns are designated as either masculine or feminine. *House*, for instance, is feminine: *la casa. Pencil*, however, is masculine: *el lapis*.

A student asked, "What gender is 'computer'?"

Instead of giving the answer, the teacher split the class into two groups, male and female, and asked them to decide for themselves whether *computer* should be a masculine or a feminine noun.

Each group was asked to give four reasons for its recommendation.

The men's group decided that *computer* should definitely be of the female gender—*la computadora*—because no one but their creator understands their internal logic; the native language they use to communicate with other computers is incomprehensible to everyone else; even the smallest mistakes are stored in long-term memory for possible retrieval later; and as soon as you make a commitment to one, you find yourself spending half your paycheck on accessories for it.

The women's group, however, concluded that computers should be masculine—*el computador*—because in order to do anything with them, you have to turn them on; they have a lot of data but still can't think for themselves; they are supposed to help you solve problems, but half the time they *are* the problem; and as soon as you commit to one, you realize that if you had waited a little longer, you could have gotten a better model.

The women won.

A Crabby Old Man

When an old man dies in the geriatric ward of a small hospital nears Tampa, Florida, It was believed that he had nothing left of any value. Later, when the nurses were going through his meager possessions, they found this poem. Its quality and content so impressed the staff that copies were made and distributed to every nurse in the hospital.

What do you see, nurses? What do you see?
What are you thinking... when you are looking at me?
A crabby old man, not very wise.
Uncertain of habit with faraway eyes?
Who dribbles his food and makes no reply.
When you say in a loud voice, "I do wish you would try!"
Who seems not to notice the things that you do.
And forever is losing a sock or a shoe?
Who, resisting or not, lets you do as you will
With bathing and feeding, the long day to fill?
Is that what you are thinking? Is that what you see?
Then open your eyes, nurse. You are not looking at me.
I'll tell you who I am, as I sit here so still.
As I do your bidding, as I eat at your will.
I am a small child of ten with a father and a mother.
Brothers and sisters who love one another,
A young boy of sixteen with wings on his feet,
Dreaming that soon now, a lover he will meet.
A groom soon at twenty, my heart gives a leap,
Remembering the vows that I promised to keep.
At twenty-five now, I have young of my own,

Who need me to guide them and a secure happy home.
A man of thirty, my young now grown fast,
Bound to each other, with ties that should last.
At forty, my young sons have grown and are gone,
But my woman's beside me to see I do not mourn.
At fifty once more, babies play 'round my knee,
Again we know children, my loved one and me.

Dark days are upon me. My wife is dead.
I look at the future; I shudder with dread.
For my young are all rearing young of their own,
And I think of the years, and the love I have known.
I am now and old man—and nature is cruel;
'Tis jest to make old age look like a fool.
The body, it crumbles; grace and vigor depart,
There is now a stone
Where once I had a heart.

But inside this old carcass, a young guy still dwells,
And now and again, my battered heart swells.
I remember the joys; I remember the pain.
And I am loving and living
Life over again.
I think of the years
All too few, gone too fast,
And accept the stark fact
That nothing can last.
So open your eyes, people
Open and see,
Not a crabby old man
Look closer.
See *me*!

Remember this poem when you next meet an older person whom you might brush aside without looking at the young soul within. We will all, one day, be there too!

People Come into Your Life for a Reason

People come into your life for a reason, a season, or a lifetime. When you know which one it is, you will know what to do for that person.

When someone is in your life for a *reason*, it is usually to meet a need you have expressed. They come to assist you through a difficulty, to provide you with guidance and support, to aid you physically, emotionally or spiritually.

This may seem like a godsend, and they are. They are there for the reason you need them to be. Then, without any wrongdoing on your part or at an inconvenient time, this person will say or do something to bring the relationship to an end.

Sometimes they die. Sometimes they walk away. Sometimes they act up and force you to take a stand. What we must realize is that our need has been met, our desire fulfilled, their work is done. The prayer you sent up has been answered and now it is time to move on.

Some people come into your life for a *season*, because your turn has come to share, grow, or learn. They bring you an experience of peace or make you laugh. They may teach you something you have never done. They usually give you an unbelievable amount of joy. Believe it, it is real. But only for a *season*!

Lifetime relationships teach you lifetime lessons, things you must build upon in order to have a solid emotional foundation. Your job is to accept the lesson, love the person, and put what you have learned to use in all other relationships and areas of your life. It is said that love is blind, but friendship is clairvoyant.

Thank you for being a part of my life, whether you were a *reason*, a *season*, or a *lifetime*.

To Lovable You

By T. Merton

"Love is our true destiny.
We do not find the meaning of life
By ourselves alone,
We find it with one another."

A Butterfly

A man found a cocoon for a butterfly. One day, a small opening appeared, he sat and watched the butterfly for several hours as it struggled to force its body through the little hole. Then it seemed to stop making any progress. It appeared as if it had gotten as far as it could and could go no farther. Then the man decided to help the butterfly.

He took a pair of scissors and snipped the remaining bit of the cocoon. The butterfly then emerged easily. Something was strange. The butterfly had a swollen body and shriveled wings. The man continued to watch the butterfly because he expected at any moment, the wings would enlarge and expand to be able to support the body, which would contract in time. Neither happened. In fact, the butterfly spent the rest of its life crawling around with a swollen body and deformed wings. It was never able to fly.

What the man in his kindness and haste did not understand was that the restricting cocoon and the struggle required for the butterfly to get through the small opening of the cocoon are God's way of forcing fluid from the body of the butterfly into its wings so that it would be ready for flight once it achieved its freedom from the cocoon. Sometimes struggles are exactly what we need in our life.

If we go through life without any obstacles, that would cripple us. We would not be as strong as what we could have been. Not only that, we could never fly.

A Great Living Will

I, Maxine, being of sound mind and body, do not wish to be kept alive indefinitely by artificial means. Under no circumstances should my fate be put in the hands of pinhead politicians who couldn't pass ninth grade biology if their lives depended on it, or lawyers/doctors interested in running up their bills. If a reasonable amount of time passes, and I fail to ask for at least one of the following:

a glass of wine
chocolate
margarita
martini
cold beer
chocolate
chicken fried steak
cream gravy
chocolate
french fries
chocolate
pizza
chocolate
ice cream
cup of tea
chocolate
coffee
sex
chocolate

It should be presumed that I won't ever get better. When such a determination is reached, I hereby instruct my appointed person and attending physicians to pull the plug, reel in the tubes, and just call it a day.

Slow Dance

This poem was written by a terminally ill young girl in a New York hospital.

Have you ever watched kids?
On a merry-go-round?
Or listened to the rain
Slapping on the ground?
Ever follow a butterfly's erratic flight?

Or gazed at the sun into the fading night?
You better slow down.
Don't dance so fast.
Time is short.
The music won't last.

Do you run through each day?
On the fly?
When you ask, "How are you"?
Do you hear the reply?
When the day is done.

Do you lie in your bed
With the next hundred chores
Running through your head?
You'd better slow down
Don't dance so fast.
Time is short.
The music won't last.

Ever told your child,
We'll do that tomorrow?
And in your haste,
Not see his/her sorrow?
Ever lost touch,
Let a good friendship die
'Cause you never had the time
To call and say, "Hi."
You'd better slow down.
Don't dance so fast.
The music won't last.

When you run so fast to get somewhere,
You miss half the fun of getting there
When you worry and hurry through the day.
It is like an unopened gift…
Thrown away.

Life is not a race.
Do take it slower
Hear the music
Before the song is over.

God Saw

God saw you getting tired
And a cure was not to be,
So he put his arms around you,
And whispered, "Come to me."
With tearful eyes we watched you,
And saw you pass away.
Although we loved you dearly,
We could not make you stay.
A folded heart stopped beating,
Hard working hands at rest,

—In memory of David Romer

Three Things to Think About

1. Cows.
2. The Constitution, and
3. The Commandments.

Cows

Is it just me, or does anyone else find it amazing that our government can track a single cow born in Canada almost three years ago, right to the stall where she sleeps in the state of Washington? And they tracked her calves to their stalls. But they are unable to locate eleven million illegal aliens wandering around the country. Maybe we should give each of them a cow.

The Constitution

They keep talking about drafting a constitution for Iraq. Why don't we just give them ours? It was written by a lot of really smart guys, it has worked for over two hundred years, and we're not using it anymore.

The Ten Commandments

The real reason that we cannot have the Ten Commandments posted in the courthouse is you cannot post, "Thou shall not steal," "Thou shall not commit adultery," and "Thou shall not lie" in a building full of lawyers, judges, and politicians. It creates a hostile work environment.

Confucius Says

Man who run in
Front of car get tired.

Man who run behind
Car get exhausted.

Man with one
Chopstick go hungry.

Man who scratch butt
Should not bite fingernails.

Man who eats many
Prunes get good run for money.

Baseball is wrong.
Man with four balls
Cannot walk!

War does not determine who is right,
War determines who is left.

Wife who put
Husband in doghouse
Soon find him in cathouse.

Man who fight with wife
All day get no piece at night.

Man who drive like hell,
Bound to get there.

Man who fish in other man's well
Often catch crabs.

Crowded elevator
Smell different to midget.

Upon seeing the shadow of a pigeon,
One must resist the urge to look up.

One Hundred Percent

This comes from two mathematics teachers with a combined total of seventy years of experience. This is strictly a mathematical viewpoint. It goes like this:

What makes 100 percent? What does it mean to give *more* than 100 percent? Ever wonder about those people who say they are giving more than 100 percent? We all have been to those meetings where someone wants you to give over 100 percent. How about achieving 103 percent? What up makes up 100 percent in life?

Here is a little mathematical formula that might help you answer these questions:

If
A B C D E F G H I J K L M N O P Q R S T U V W X Y Z.
Is represented as
1 2 3 4 5 6 7 8 910 11 12 13 14 151 16 17 18 19 20 21 22 23 24 25 26

Then,
H-A-R-D-W-O-R-K
8+1+18+4+23+15+18+11 = 98 percent

And,
K-N-O-W-L-E-D-G-E
11+14+15+23+12+5 +4+7+5 = 96 percent

But,
A-T-T-I-T-U-D-E
1+20+20+9+20+21+4+5 = 100 percent

And,
B-U-L-L-S-H-I-T
2+21+12+12+19+8+9+20 = 103 percent

And look how far ass-kissing will take you:
A-S-S-K-I-S-S-I-N-G
1+19+19+11+9+19+19+9+14+7 = 118 percent

So one can logically conclude with mathematical certainty, that while hard work and knowledge will get you close, and attitude will get you there, it is bullshit and ass-kissing that will put you over the top.

The Trustworthiness of a Lawyer

A mafia godfather finds out that his bookkeeper has cheated him out of ten million bucks. His bookkeeper is stone-cold deaf. That was the reason he got the job in the first place. It was assumed that a deaf bookkeeper would not hear anything that he might have to testify about in court. When the godfather goes to confront the bookkeeper about his missing ten million dollars, he brings along his attorney, who knows sign language.

The godfather tells the lawyer, "Ask him where the ten million bucks he embezzled from me is." The attorney, using sign language, asks the bookkeeper where the money is. The bookkeeper signs back, "I don't know what you are talking about."

The attorney tells the godfather, "He says he doesn't know what you are talking about."

The godfather pulls out his pistol, puts it to the bookkeeper's temple, and says, "Ask him again!"

The attorney signs to the bookkeeper, "He will kill you if you don't tell him."

The bookkeeper signs back, "Okay! You win! The money is in a brown briefcase buried behind the shed in my cousin Enzo's backyard in Queens!"

The godfather asks the attorney, "Well, what did he say?"

The attorney replies, "He says you don't have the balls to pull the trigger."

The Irish Mating Call

Two Indians and an Irishman were walking through the woods. All of a sudden, one of the Indians ran up a hill to the mouth of a small cave.

"Wooooo! Wooooo! Wooooo!" he called into the cave and listened closely until he heard an answer. "Wooooo! Wooooo! Wooooo!" He tore off his clothes and ran into the cave.

The Irishman was puzzled and asked the remaining Indian what it was all about. "Was the other Indian crazy or what?"

The Indian replied, "No, it is our custom during mating season when Indian men see the cave, they holler, 'Wooooo! Wooooo! Wooooo!' into the opening. If they get an answer back, it means there is a beautiful squaw in there waiting for us."

Just then, they came upon another cave. The second Indian ran up to the cave, stopped, and hollered, Wooooo! Wooooo! Wooooo! from deep inside.

He also tore off his clothes and ran into the opening.

The Irishman wandered around the woods alone for a while, and then spied a third large cave. As he looked in amazement at the size of the opening, he was thinking, "Look at the size of this cave! It is bigger than those found by the Indians."

There must be some really big, fine women in this cave! He stood in front of the opening and hollered with all of his might, "Wooooo! Wooooo! Wooooo!" Like the others, he then heard an answering call, "WOOOOOOOOO! WOOOOOOOOO! WOOOOOOOOO!"

With a gleam in his eye and a smile on his face, he raced into the cave, tearing off his clothes as he ran.

The following day, the headline of the local newspaper read... you'll like this: NAKED IRISHMAN RUN OVER BY TRAIN.

The Value of a Catholic Education and a No. 2 Pencil

Little Susie was not the best student in the Catholic school. Usually, she slept through the class.

One day, her teacher, a nun, called on her while she was sleeping. "Tell me, Susie, who created the universe? When Susie did not stir, Little Johnny, who was her friend sitting behind her, took his pencil and jabbed her in the rear.

"God Almighty!" shouted Susie.

The nun replied, "Very good!" And Susie fell back to sleep.

A little later, the nun asked Susie, "Who is our Lord and Savior?"

Susie didn't stir from her slumber. Once again, Johnny came to her rescue and stuck her in the butt with the pencil.

"Jesus Christ!" shouted Susie.

And the nun once again said, "Very good," and Susie fell back to sleep.

The nun asked her a third question. "What did Eve say to Adam after she had her twenty-third child?"

Again, Johnny came to the rescue. This time, however, Susie jumped up and shouted, "If you stick that thing in me one more time, I'll break it in half!"

The nun fainted.

You Might Be a School Employee

You might be a school employee if you believe the playground should be equipped with a Ritalin salt lick.

You might be a school employee if you want to slap the next person who says, "Must be nice to work eight to three thirty and have the summers off."

You might be a school employee if you know how many days, minutes, and seconds there are in a school year.

You might be a school employee if it is difficult to name your own child because there is not a name you can come up with that doesn't bring high blood pressure as it is uttered.

You might be a school employee if you can tell it's a full moon or if it's going to rain, snow, or hail without looking outside.

You might be a school employee if you believe shallow gene pool should have its own box on the report card.

You might be a school employee if you believe that unspeakable evils will befall you if anyone says, "Boy, the kids are sure mellow today."

You might be a school employee if when out in public, you feel the urge to snap your fingers at children you do not know and correct their behavior.

You might be a school employee if you have no social life between August and June.

You might be a school employee if you think people should have a government permit before being allowed to reproduce.

You might be a school employee if you wonder how some parents *managed* to reproduce.

You might be a school employee if you laugh uncontrollably when people refer to the staff room as the "lounge."

You might be a school employee if after meeting a child's parent instant answers this question, "Why is this kid like this?"

You might be a school employee if you choose a mammogram over a parental conference.

You might be a school employee if the words, "I have college debt for this?" has ever come out of your mouth.

How Smart Is Your Right Foot?

You have to try this. It only takes two seconds.

Without anyone watching you (they may seek immediate help for you), and while sitting at your desk in front of your computer, lift your right foot off the floor and make clockwise circles.

Now, while doing this, draw the number six in the air with your right hand.

Your foot will change direction. I told you so!

And there is nothing you can do about it.

You and I both know how stupid it is, but before the day is done, you are going to try this again—if you have not already done so.

Why Italians Can't Be Paramedics

Vinny and Tony are out in the woods hunting when suddenly, Tony grabs his chest and falls to the ground. He doesn't seem to be breathing; his eyes are rolled back in his head.

Vinny whips out his cell phone and calls 911. He gasps to the operator, "I think Tony is dead! What should I do?"

"First, let's make sure he is dead."

There is silence, and then a shot is heard.

Vinnie's voice comes back on line, "Okay, now what?"

A Lucky Day

She was standing in the kitchen preparing to boil eggs for breakfast, wearing only the T-shirt that she normally slept in.

As I walked into the kitchen, not quite fully awake, she turned and said softly, "You've got to make love to me at this very moment."

My eyes lit up, and I thought, "I am either still dreaming or this is going to be my lucky day."

Not wanting to lose the moment, I embraced her and gave it my all right there on the kitchen table.

Afterwards, she said, "Thanks." And then she returned to the stove. Her T-shirt was still around her neck.

A little puzzled, I asked, "What was that all about?"

She explained, "The egg timer's broken."

A Remarkable Obituary

Today, we mourn the passing of a beloved old friend, Mr. Common Sense.

Mr. Sense had been with us for many years. No one knows for sure how old he was, since his birth records were long ago lost in bureaucratic red tape.

He will be remembered as having cultivated such valued lessons as knowing when to come in out of the rain, why the early bird gets the worm, and that life is not always fair.

Common Sense lived by a simple, sound financial policy ("do not spend more than you earn") and reliable parenting strategies ("adults, not kids, are in charge.")

His health began to rapidly deteriorate when well-intentioned but overbearing regulations were set in place. Reports of a six-year-old boy charged with sexual harassment for kissing a classmate; teens suspended from school for using mouthwash after lunch; and a teacher fired for reprimanding an unruly student, only worsened this condition.

Mr. Sense declined even further when schools were required to get parental consent to administer aspirin to a student but could not inform the parents when a student became pregnant and wanted to have an abortion.

Finally, Common Sense lost the will to live as the Ten Commandments became contraband, churches became businesses, and criminals received better treatment than their victims.

Common Sense finally gave up the ghost after a woman failed to realize that a steaming cup of coffee was hot, spilled it in her lap, and was awarded a huge financial settlement.

Common Sense was preceded in death by his parents, Truth and Trust; his wife, Discretion; his daughter, Responsibility; and his son, Reason. He is survived by two stepbrothers: My Rights and Ima Whiner.

Not many attended his funeral because so few realized he was gone. If you still remember him, pass this on; if not, join the majority and do nothing.

Would the congress and the president please acknowledge?

Retirement in Maine

Tom had been in the liquor business for twenty-five years. Finally, sick of the stress, he quits his job, and buys fifty acres of land in Maine as far away from humanity as he could get.

He sees the postman once a week and gets groceries once a month. Otherwise, it is total peace and quiet.

After six months or so of almost total isolation, someone knocks on his door. He opens it, and a huge bearded man is standing there.

"Name's Ephus, your neighbor from forty miles up the road. Having a Christmas party Friday night. Thought you might like to come. About five thirty."

"Great," says Tom, "after six months out here, I'm ready to meet some local folks. Thank you."

As Ephus is leaving, he stops. "Got to warn you, there will be some drinking."

"Not a problem," says Tom. "After twenty-five years in the business, I can drink with the best of 'em."

Again, the big man starts to leave and stops, "More 'n likely gonna be some fightin' too."

"Well, I get along with people, I'll be all right. I'll be there. Thanks again."

"More 'n likely be some wild sex too."

"Now that's really not a problem," says Tom, warming to the idea. "I've been all alone for six months! I'll definitely be there. By the way, what should I wear?"

"Don't much matter. Just gonna be the two of us."

A Lesson Plan to Remember

Back in September 2005, on the first day of school, Martha Cothren, a social studies school teacher at Robinson High School in Little Rock, Alabama, did something not to be forgotten. On the first day of school, with the permission of the school superintendent, the principal, and the building supervisor, she removed all of the desks out of her classroom. When the first period kids entered the room, they discovered that there were no desks.

Looking around, confused, they asked, "Mrs. Cothren, where are our desks?"

She replied, "You can't have a desk until you tell me what you have done to earn the right to sit at a desk."

They thought, "Well, maybe it's our grades."

"No," she said.

"Maybe it is our behavior."

She told them, "No, it's not even your behavior."

And so, they came and went, the first period, second period, third period. Still no desks in the classroom. By early afternoon, television news crews had started gathering in Mrs. Cothren's classroom to report about this crazy teacher who had taken all the desks out of her room.

The final period of the day came, and as puzzled students found seats on the floor of the desk-less classroom, Martha Cothren said, "Throughout the day, no one has been able to tell me just what he/she has done to earn the right to sit at the desks that are ordinarily found in this classroom. Now I am going to tell you."

At this point, Martha Cothern went over to the door of her classroom and opened it. Twenty-seven U.S. Veterans, all in uniforms, walked into the classroom, each one carrying a school desk. The vets began placing the school desks in rows, and then they would walk over and stand alongside the wall.

By the time the last solider had set the final desk in place, those kids started to understand, perhaps for the first time in their lives, just how the right to sit at those desks had been earned.

Martha said, "You didn't earn the right to sit at these desks. These heroes did it for you. They placed the desks here for you. Now, it's up to you to sit in them. It is your responsibility to learn, to be good students, to be good citizens. They paid the price so that you could have the freedom to get an education. Don't ever forget it!"

Ten Powerful Lessons of High-Performing Schools

1. They focus on what they *can* do, rather than what they *can't*.
2. They don't leave anything about teaching and learning to chance.
3. They set their goals high.
4. Higher-performing secondary schools put all kids—not just some—in a demanding high school core curriculum.
5. High-performing schools are obsessive about time, especially instructional time.
6. Principals are hugely important, ever present, *not* the only leaders in the school.
7. Good schools know how much teachers matter, and they act on that knowledge.
8. They are obsessive about data.
9. They are nice places for both teachers and students.
10. They never back down.

—Katie Haycock, 2007
Springfield, MA Public Schools

The Woman Golfer

A woman golfer was out golfing one day when she hit her ball into the woods. She went into the woods to look for it and found a frog in a sand trap.

The frog said to her, "If you release me from this trap, I will grant you three wishes."

The woman freed the frog, and the frog said, "Thank you, but I failed to mention that there was a condition to your wishes. Whatever you wish for, your husband will get ten times!"

The woman said. "That's okay!"

For her first wish, she wanted to be the most beautiful woman in the world. The frog warned her, "You realize that this wish will also make your husband the most handsome man in the world, an Adonis whom women will flock to."

The woman replied, "That's okay, because I will be the most beautiful woman and he will have eyes for only me."

So *kazam*, she is now the most beautiful woman in the world!

For her second wish, she wanted to be the richest woman in the world.

The frog said, "That will make your husband the richest man in the world. And he will be ten times richer than you."

The woman said, 'That's okay because what's mine is his, and what's his is mine."

So *kazam*, she is the richest woman in the world!

The frog then inquired about her third wish, and she answered, "I'd like a mild heart attack."

Moral of the story: Women are clever. Do not mess with them.
Ah, but the man had a heart attack ten times milder than his wife.
Moral of the story: Women think they are really smart.

Comments Made in the Year 1955

"No one can afford to get sick anymore, at fifteen dollars a day in the hospital, it's too rich for my blood."

"I'll tell you one thing, if things keep going the way they are, it's going to be impossible to buy a week's groceries for ten dollars."

"Have you seen the new cars coming out next year? It won't be long before one thousand dollars will only buy a used one."

"If cigarettes keep going up in price, I'm going to quit. Twenty cents a pack is ridiculous."

"Did you hear the post office is thinking about charging seven cents just to mail a letter?"

"If they raise the minimum wage to one dollar, nobody will be able to hire outside help at the store."

"When I first started driving, who would have thought gas would someday cost twenty-five cents a gallon. Guess we'd be better off leaving the car in the garage."

"I'm afraid to send my kids to the movies any more. Ever since they let Clark Gable get by saying *damn* in *Gone with the Wind*, it seems every new movie has either *hell* or *damn* in it."

"I read the other day where scientists think it is possible to put a man on the moon by the end of the century. They even have some fellows they call astronauts preparing for it down in Texas."

"Did you see where some baseball player just signed for fifty thousand dollars a year just to play ball? It wouldn't surprise me if someday they'll be making more than the president."

"I never thought I'd see the day all our kitchen appliances would be electric. They are even making electric typewriters now."

"It's too bad things are so tough nowadays. I see where a few married women are having to work to make ends meet."

"It won't be long before young couples are going to have to hire someone to watch their kids so they can both work."

"Thank goodness I won't live to see the day when the government takes half our income in taxes. I sometimes wonder if we are electing the best people to government."

"The drive-in restaurant is convenient in nice weather, but I seriously doubt they will ever catch on."

What I Have Learned

The less time I have to work, the more things I get done.

That under everyone's hard shell is someone who wants to be appreciated and loved.

The Lord didn't do it all in one day. What makes me think I can?

Money does not buy class.

That it is those small daily happenings that make life so spectacular.

Life is like a roll of toilet paper. The closer it gets to the end, the faster it goes.

We should be glad God does not give us everything we ask for.

The following are from Psalm 90:12: "Teach us to make the most of our time so that we may grow in wisdom."

Take time to think—it is the source of power.

Take time to play—it is the secret of perpetual youth.

Take time to read—it is the foundation of wisdom.

Take time to pray—it is the greatest power on earth.

Take time to be friendly—it is the road to happiness.

Take time to give—it is too short a day to be selfish.

Take time to be excellent—it does not happen by chance

Take time to work—it is the price of success

Take time to love and be loved—it is a God-given privilege.

For Those Who Thought They Knew Everything

The liquid inside coconuts can be used as a substitute for blood plasma.

No piece of paper can be folded in half more than seven times.

Donkeys kill more people annually than plane crashes or shark attacks. So you had better watch your *ass*.

You burn more calories sleeping than you do watching television.

Oak trees do not produce acorns until they are fifty years of age or older.

The first product to have a barcode was Wrigley's gum.

The King of Hearts is the only king without a moustache.

American Airlines saved forty thousand dollars in 1987 by eliminating one olive from each salad served in first class.

Venus is the only planet that rotates clockwise. Since Venus is normally associated with women, what does that tell you?

Apples, not caffeine, are more efficient at waking you up in the morning.

Most dust particles in your house are made from dead skin.

The first owner of the Marlboro cigarette company dies from lung cancer, as did the first Marlboro man.

Walt Disney was afraid of mice.

Pearls dissolve in vinegar.

The three most valuable brand names on earth, in order are: Marlboro, Coca-Cola, and Budweiser.

It is possible to lead a cow upstairs but not downstairs.

Dentists have recommended that a toothbrush be kept at least six feet away from a toilet to avoid airborne particles resulting from the flush.

And the best for last: Turtles can breathe through their butts. I know some people like that, don't you?

Do Not Mess With Little Kids

A little girl was talking to her teacher about whales. The teacher said it was physically impossible for a whale to swallow a human because even though it was a very large mammal, its throat was very small. The little girl stated that Jonah was swallowed by a whale. Irritated, the teacher reiterated that a whale could not swallow a human; it was physically impossible.

The little girl said, "When I get to heaven, I will ask Jonah."

The teacher asked, "What if Jonah went to hell?"

The little girl replied, "Then you ask him."

A Sunday school teacher was discussing the Ten Commandments with her five- and six-year-olds. After explaining the commandment to honor thy father and thy mother, she asked, "Is there a commandment that teaches us how to treat our brothers and sisters?"

Without missing a beat, one little boy (the oldest in his family) answered, "Thou shall not kill."

One day, a little girl was sitting and watching her mother do the dishes at the kitchen sink. She suddenly noticed that her mother had several strands of white hair sticking out in contrast on her brunette head. She looked at her mother and asked, "Why are some of your hairs white, Mom?"

Her mother replied, "Well, every time that you do something wrong and make me cry or unhappy, one of my hairs turns white."

The little girl thought about this revelation for a while and then said, "Mamma, how come *all* of Grandma's hairs are white?"

The children had all been photographed. And the teacher was trying to persuade them each to buy a copy of the group picture. "Just think of how nice it will be to look at it when you are all grown up and say, 'There's Jennifer, she's a lawyer,' or 'that's Michael, he's a doctor.'"

A small voice from the back of the room rang out, "And there's the teacher, she's dead."

The children were lined up in the cafeteria of a Catholic elementary school for lunch. At the head of the table was a large pile of apples. The nun made a note and posted on the apple tray: "Take only one. God is watching."

Moving farther along the lunch line, at the other end of the table, was a large pile of chocolate chip cookies. A child had written this note, "Take all you want. God is watching the apples."

A teacher was giving a lesson on the circulation of the blood. Trying to make the matter clearer, she said, "Now, class, if I stood on my head, the blood, as you know, would run to my head. And I would turn red in the face."

"Yes," the class said.

"Then why is it that while I am standing upright in the ordinary position, the blood doesn't run into my feet?"

A little voice from the back shouted, "Because your feet ain't empty?"

The Magic of Believing

by Edward J. McGrath Jr.

I am not old enough to play baseball
Or football. I am not eight yet.
My mom told me when you start baseball,
You aren't going to be able to run
That fast because you had an operation.
I told Mom I wouldn't need to run
That fast.
When I play baseball,
I'll just hit them out of the park,
Then I'll be able to walk.

Where Are the Heroes?

"Where are the heroes of today?" a radio talk show host thundered.

He blames society's shortcomings on education. Too many people are looking for heroes in all the wrong places. Movie stars and rock musicians, athletes, and models aren't heroes; they are celebrities.

Heroes abound in public schools, a fact that doesn't make the news. There is no precedent for the level of violence, drugs, broken homes, child abuse, and crime in today's America. Education didn't create these problems but deals with them every day. Hello, you high stakes, silver-spooned liberal educators? When is the last time you dealt with that many problems or have you been too busy trying to correct false perceptions in education and apply a business attitude toward education? Vultures, you are no better than subversive groups in the forties and fifties and politicians like Joe McCarthy.

You want heroes? You want heroes? Consider Dave Sanders, the schoolteacher shot to death while trying to shield his students from two youths on a shooting rampage at Columbine High School in Littleton, Colorado. Sanders gave his life, along with twelve students, and other less heralded heroes survived the Colorado blood bath.

You want heroes? You want heroes? Jane Smith, a Fayetteville, North Carolina, teacher was moved by the plight of her students, a boy dying for want of a kidney transplant. So this woman told the family of a fourteen-year-old boy that she would give him one of her kidneys. And she did. When they subsequently appeared together hugging on the *Today Show*, even Katie Couric was near tears.

You want heroes? You want heroes? Doris Dillon dreamed all her life of being a teacher. She not only made it; she was one of those wondrous teachers who could bring out the best in every single student who touched her life. One of her fellow teachers in San Jose, California, said, "She could teach a rock to read." Suddenly, she was stricken with Lou Gehrig's disease—which is always fatal, usually within five years. She asked to stay on the job—and did. When her voice was affected, she communicated with a computer. Did she go home? Absolutely not! When the disease was diagnosed, she wrote the staff and all the families that she had one last lesson to teach, that dying was part of living. Her colleagues named her Teacher of the Year.

Hey, you high-priced politicians who get the best of the best and tell us we have to carry more water up the hill!

You want heroes? You want heroes? Bob House, a teacher in Gay, Georgia, tried out for *Who Wants to be a Millionaire*. After he won a million dollars, a network film crew wanted to follow up to see how it impacted his life. New cars? Big house? Jewelry? Instead, they found both Bob House and his wife still teaching. They explained that it was what they had always wanted to do with their lives, and that would not change. The community was both stunned and gratified

You want heroes? You want heroes? Last year, the average teacher spent $468 of their own money for student necessities—workbooks, pencils, supplies for kids had to have but could not afford. Hey, you state boards of education and governors, Washington legislators, are you really listening to the voices of the country you are supposedly representing? That is a lot of money from the pockets of the most poorly paid teachers in the industrial world.

You want heroes? You want heroes? Public education provides more Sunday school teachers than any profession, including legislators if in fact there are any moral people in the legislature. The average teacher works more hours in nine months than the average forty-hour employee does in a year.

You want heroes? You want heroes? For millions of kids, the hug they get from a teacher is the only hug they get that day because the nation is living through the worst parenting in history. An Argyle, Texas, kindergarten teacher hugs her little five- and six-year-olds so much that both the boys and girls run up and hug her when they see her in the hall, at the football games, or in the malls years later.

You want heroes? You want heroes? A Michigan principal moved an author to tears with the story of her attempt to rescue a badly abused little boy who doted on a stuffed animal on her desk. One that said, "I love you." He had never been told that at home. This is a constant in today's society—two million unwanted, unloved, abused children in the public schools, the only institution that takes them all in and cares for them.

You want heroes? You want heroes? Visit a special education classroom and watch the miracle of personal interaction, a job so difficult that fellow teachers are in awe by the dedication they witness. There is a sentence from an unnamed source which says, "We have been so eager to give our children what we did not have that we have neglected to give them what we did."

You want heroes? You want heroes? Then go down to your local school and see our real live heroes, the ones changing lives for the better each and every day!

Wit and Wisdom from Will Rogers

Never slap a man who's chewing tobacco.

Never kick a cow chip on a hot day.

There are two theories to arguing with a woman—neither works.

Never miss a chance to shut up.

Always drink upstream from the herd.

If you find yourself in a hole, stop digging.

The quickest way to double your money is to fold it and put it back in your pocket.

There are three kinds of men: The ones that learn by reading; the few who learn by observation; the rest of them have to pee on an electric fence to find out for themselves.

Good judgment comes from experience, and a lot of that comes from bad judgment.

If you're riding ahead of the herd, take a look back every now and then to make sure it's still there.

Lettin' the cat eat outta the bag is a whole lot easier 'n puttin' it back.

After eating an entire bull, a mountain lion felt so good he started roaming. He kept it up until a hunter came along and shot him. The moral: When you're full of bull, keep your mouth shut.

Let's Play 21

ONE. Give people more than they expect cheerfully.

TWO. Marry a man or woman you love to talk to. As you get older, their conversation skills will be as important as any other.

THREE. Don't believe all you hear. Spend all you have or sleep all you want.

FOUR. When you say, "I love you," mean it.

FIVE. When you say, "I'm sorry," look the person right in the eye.

SIX. Be engaged at least six months before you get married.

SEVEN. Believe in love at first sight.

EIGHT. Never laugh at anyone's dream. People who don't have dreams don't have much.

NINE. Love deeply and passionately. You might get hurt, but it's the only way to live your life.

TEN. In disagreements, fight fairly. No name calling.

ELEVEN. Don't judge people by their relatives.

TWELVE. Talk slowly but think quickly.

THIRTEEN. When someone asks you a question you don't want to answer, smile and ask, "Why do you want to know?"

FOURTEEN. Remember that great love and great achievements involve great risk.

FIFTEEN. Say "God bless you" when you hear someone sneeze.

SIXTEEN. When you lose, don't lose the lesson.

SEVENTEEN. Remember the three Rs: respect for self; respect for others; and responsibility for all your actions.

EIGHTEEN. Don't let a little dispute injure a great friendship.

NINETEEN. When you realize you've made a mistake, take immediate steps to correct it.

TWENTY. Smile when picking up the phone, the caller will hear it in your voice.

TWENTY-ONE. Spend some time alone.

The Wooden Bowl

I guarantee you will remember the tale of the Wooden Bowl tomorrow, a week from now, a month from now, and a year from now.

A frail old man went to live with his son, daughter-in-law, and four-year-old grandson. The old man's hands trembled, his eyesight blurred, and his step faltered. The family ate together at the table.

The elderly grandfather's shaky hands and failing sight made eating difficult. Peas rolled off his spoon and onto the floor. When he grasped the glass, milk spilled on the tablecloth.

The son and daughter-in-law became irritated with the mess. "We must do something about father," said the son. "I've had enough of his spilled milk, noisy eating, and food on the floor." So the husband and wife set a small table in the corner of the kitchen. There, grandfather ate alone while the rest of the family enjoyed dinner. Since grandfather had broken a dish or two, his food was served in a wooden bowl!

When the family glanced in grandfather's direction, sometimes he had a tear in his eye as he sat alone. Still, the only words the couple had for him were sharp admonitions when he dropped a fork or spilled food.

The four-year-old watched it all in silence. One evening, before supper, the father noticed his son playing with wood scraps on the floor. He asked the child sweetly, "What are you making?"

Just as sweetly, the boy replied, "Oh, I am making a little bowl for you and Mama to eat your food in when I grow up." The four-year-old smiled and went back to work.

The words so struck the parents, they were speechless. Then tears started to stream down their cheeks. Though no word was spoken, both knew what had to be done. That evening, the husband took the grandfather's hand and gently led him back to the family table. For the remainder of his days, he ate every meal with the family; and for some reason, neither the husband nor the wife seemed to care when a fork was dropped, milk spilled, or the tablecloth soiled.

I've learned that no matter what happens, how bad it seems today, life does go on—and it will be better tomorrow.

I've learned you can tell a lot about a person by the way he/she handles four things: a rainy day, the elderly, lost luggage, and tangled Christmas tree lights.

I've learned that regardless of your relationship with your parents, you'll miss them when they are gone from your life.

I've learned that life sometimes gives you a second chance.

I've learned that making a living is not the same as making a life.

Senior Pension

Seniors, are you worried that your pension will run short? Well, not to worry. There is a solution.

Senior Health Care Solution

So you are a sick senior citizen, and the government says there is no nursing home available for you, what do you do? Our plan gives anyone sixty-five years or older a gun and four bullets. You are allowed to shoot two congressmen and two illegal immigrants.

Of course, this means you will be sent to prison; however, when you get there, you will get three meals a day, a roof over your head, central heating, air-conditioning, and all the health care you need.

Need glasses, you'll get them. New hip, knees, kidney, lungs, heart? All covered (And your kids can come and visit you as often as they do now).

Who will be paying for all of this? The same government that just told you that they cannot afford for you go into a home. Plus (get this) because you are a prisoner, you do not have to pay income taxes anymore.

Is this a great country or what!

The Wrong E-mail Address

This is a lesson to be learned by typing in the wrong e-mail address.

A Minneapolis couple decided to go to Florida to thaw out during a particularly icy winter. They planned to stay at the same hotel where they spent their honeymoon twenty years earlier.

Because of hectic schedules, it was difficult to coordinate their travel schedules. So the husband left Minnesota and flew to Florida on Thursday, with his wife flying down the following day.

The husband checked into the hotel. There was a computer in his room, so he decided to send an e-mail to his wife. However, he accidentally left out one letter in her e-mail address, and without realizing his error, he sent the e-mail.

Meanwhile, somewhere in Houston, a widow had just returned home from her husband's funeral. He was a minister who was called home to glory following a heart attack.

The widow decided to check her e-mail, expecting messages from relatives and friends. After reading the first message, she screamed and fainted. The widow's son rushed into the room, found his mother on the floor, and saw the computer screen, which read the following:

> To: My loving wife
> Subject: I've just arrived
> Date: October 16, 2009

I know you are surprised to hear from me. They have computers here now, and you are allowed to send e-mails to your loved ones. I've just arrived and have checked in.

I've seen that everything has been prepared for your arrival tomorrow. Looking forward to seeing you then! Hope your journey is as uneventful as mine was.

P.S. Sure is freaking hot down here!

A Wife Making Breakfast

A wife was making a breakfast of fried eggs for her husband. Suddenly, her husband burst into the kitchen.

"Careful! Careful! Put in some more butter! Oh my god! You are cooking too many at once. Too many! Turn them! Turn them now! We need more butter! Oh my god! Where are we going to get more butter? They are going to stick! Careful! Careful! I said careful! You never listen to me when you are cooking! Never! Turn them! Hurry up! Are you crazy? Have you lost your mind? Don't forget to salt them. Use the salt. Use the salt! Use the salt!"

The wife stared at him and said, "What the hell is wrong with you? You think I don't know how to fry a couple of eggs?"

The husband calmly replied, "I wanted to show you what it feels like when I am driving!"

Do You Remember When...

All the girls had ugly gym uniforms?

It took five minutes for the TV to warm up?

Nearly everyone's mom was at home when the kids got home from school?

When a quarter was a decent allowance?

Your mom wore nylons that came in two pieces?

Your male teachers wore neckties, and the female teachers wore high heels.

Your windshield was cleaned, oil checked, and gas was pumped all for free?

They threatened to keep kids back a grade if they failed?

No one ever asked where the car keys were because they were always in the ignition, and the doors were never locked.

Lying on your back in the grass with your friends and saying things like, "That cloud looks like a..." And playing baseball in a sandlot with no adults to help kids with the rules of the game?

When the '57 Chevy was everyone's dream car?

When being sent to the principal's office was nothing compared to the fate that awaited the student at home?

And with all the progress, don't you just wish—just once—you could slip back in time and savor the slower pace and share it with the children of today?

Summers filled with bike rides, baseball games, hula hoops, bowling, and visits to the pool, and eating Kool-Aid powder with sugar. Didn't that feel good to go back and say, "Yeah, I remember that"?

A Eulogy

To my sister

Reverend clergy, friends, and family. God puts us all in one another's lives to impact one another in some way. Always look for God in others. The best and most beautiful things cannot be seen or touched, rather they must be felt with the heart.

That is why today is a most difficult day in my life. I am not just committing my sister's body to the earth, but I am losing my best friend.

I remember how proud my mom and dad were of Phyllis and me, and that same love and caring was showered upon her three children—Cheryl, John, and David as well as their children whom she loved very much. She loved both my sons, their wives, and our children. To us, the living, this is an exceptionally difficult time because those who loved her feel the hurt and the loss.

In times of despair, a family provides the tranquility every individual must have amidst the dysfunction that is society today. It further provides each member a sense of belonging and calmness that can never be replicated and cannot be taken away by the naysayers and hucksters who prey on a person's soul. Inner strength and purpose is taught through the church and then reinforced by the family. That is who my sister is, and of whom I am very proud!

This church, our religion puts me at ease because Catholic priests understand so much better how to handle people in difficult times like this. To me, Randolph and St. Mary's will always be home.

Phyllis made the impossible possible because of her drive and determination; however, she allowed her children to grow up to be productive citizens, but it was not without some long—and I assume, loud—discussions. You know my sister may have sometimes lost her temper, so glad she never, ever, ever did that to me.

She never worshipped money. She would give you her last dollar and tell you not to worry, just have a good time. If you were her friend, you had a friend for life who was there for you when you needed her. She gave you hope and was someone to listen to you even if there was no solution. I believe that she would have said, "Friends are like flowers, they never fade, rather they are evergreen."

My sister would always tell me my mother liked me better than her, but that was because she had my dad wrapped around her little finger. I would then acknowledge her as my older sister, and she would have a comment for that which cannot be heard in church. I know we both declared that flowers made us feel nervous at our ages when we passed by them.

I remember when my mother passed, and we sat and talked about many things including death. At that time, we both agreed that was not an option and agreed to dispense the items my mother had simply so there would be no problems. I do not know if God the Father and Jesus are ready for Phyllis, but they had better bring their A-game when they meet. Of this I am sure, she will be most happy to be with Al Rodd once again. He made her whole, and she him in many ways. I believe she is in a better place now; it is our loss that hurts the heart.

If I Knew

If I knew it should be the last time
That I'd see you fall asleep,
I would tuck you in more lightly
And pray the Lord, your soul to keep.

If I knew it should be the last time
That I'd see you walk out the door,
I should give you a hug and a kiss

And call you back for one more.

If I knew it should be the last time
I'd hear your voice lifted up in praise,
I would video tape each action and word
As I could play them back day after day.

If I knew it would be the last time,
I should spare an extra minute
To stop and say, "I love you,"
Instead of assuming you should know I do.

If I knew it should be the last time,
I would be there to share your day.
Well, I'm sure you'll have so many more,
As I can let just this one slip away.

For surely there is always a tomorrow
To make up for an oversight
And we always get a second chance
To make everything right.

There will always be another day
To say, "I love you,"
And certainly there's another chance
To say, "Anything I can do?"

Tomorrow is not promised to anyone,
Young or old alike,
And today may be their last chance.

Would you please join with me in closing your eyes and remember that image of my sister you have. I will wager, we will all be very close.

In closing, there is certain connectivity between husband and wife, parents and children that creates a bond for life that never dies; blood is always thicker than water. The images, the great stories (not just good) seem to bring about fond memories of days gone by that are still fresh and vibrant in people's minds. Do not be afraid of dying; be afraid of not living life to its fullest.

> "Memories like the corners of my mind,
> Mostly watercolor memories of the way we were
> Scattered pictures of the smiles we left behind
> Smiles we gave to one another for the way we were."

The body may not be with us, but the spirit and memories will always be in the heart.

Today is yesterday once again as we celebrate the life of Phyllis Denise Hamelburg. Thank you all for sharing my sister in life. Like Phyllis, you are all beautiful people.

(Just a footnote. During the eulogies, the phone rang in the church and for that moment...)

Ronald Reagan Quotes

Listen

"Socialism only works in two places: heaven, where they don't need it; and hell, where they already have it."

"The most terrifying words in the English language are 'I'm from the government, and I am here to help.'"

"The trouble with our liberal friends is not that they are ignorant, it is just that they know so much that isn't so."

"I have wondered at times what the Ten Commandments would have looked like if Moses had to run them through the U.S. Congress."

"Of the four wars in my lifetime, none came about because the U.S. was too strong."

"The taxpayer, that is someone who works for the federal government but doesn't have to take the civil service examination."

"Government is like a baby, an alimentary canal with a big appetite at one end and no sense of responsibility."

"The nearest thing to eternal life we will ever see on this earth is a government program."

"It has been said that politics is the second oldest profession. I have learned that it bears a striking resemblance to the first."

"Government's view of the economy could be summed up in a few short phrases: if it moves, tax it. If it keeps on moving, regulate it; and if it stops moving, subsidize it."

"Less we ever forget, that we're on nation under God, then we will be one nation gone under."

The Older We Get

One

Recently, when I went to McDonald's, I saw on the menu that you could have an order of six, nine, or twelve Chicken McNuggets.

I asked for a half-dozen nuggets.

"We don't have half-dozen nuggets," said the teenager at the counter.

"You don't?" I replied.

"We only have six, nine, or twelve" was the reply.

Read this now. "So I can't order a half dozen, but I can order six?"

"That's right."

So I shook my head and ordered six McNuggets.

Unbelievable but sadly true. (Must have been the same one I asked for sweetener, and she said they didn't have any, only Splenda and sugar.)

Two

A woman at work was seen putting her credit card into her floppy drive and then pulling it out very quickly.

When I inquired as to what she was doing, she said she was shopping on the Internet, and they kept asking for a credit card number, so she was using the ATM thingy.

Keep shuddering!

Three

I was checking out at the local Wal-Mart with just a few items, and the lady behind me put her things on the belt close to my items.

I picked up of those "dividers" that they keep by the cash register and placed it between our things so they would not get mixed up.

After the girl had scanned all of my items, she picked up the "divider," looking it all over for the bar code so she could scan it. Not finding the bar code, I said to her, "I've changed my mind. I don't think I will buy that today."

She said okay, and I paid her for the things and left.

She had no clue to what had just happened.

Four

I recently saw a distraught young lady weeping beside her car. "Do you need some help?" I asked.

She replied, "I knew I should have replaced the battery to this remote door unlocker. Now I can't get into my car. Do you think (pointing to a distant convenience store) they would have a battery to fit this?"

"Hmmm, I don't know. Do you have an alarm too?" I asked.

"No, just this remote thingy," she answered, handing me her keys to the car.

As I took the key and manually opened the door, I replied, "Why don't you drive over there and check about the batteries. It is a long walk…"

Please lie down before you hurt yourself!

Five

Several years ago, we had an intern who was not particularly swift. One day, she was typing and turned to a secretary and said, "I am almost out of typing paper, what do I do?"

"Just use paper from the photocopier, the secretary told her."

With that, the intern took her last remaining blank piece of paper, put it on the photocopier and proceeded to make five blank copies.

Brunette, by the way!

Six

A mother calls 911, very worried, asking the dispatcher if she needs to take her kid to the hospital emergency room. The kid had eaten ants. The dispatcher tells her to give the kid some Benadryl, and he should be fine, the mother says, "I just gave him some ant killer—"

The dispatcher said, "Rush him to the hospital."

Life is tough. It's even tougher if you are stupid!

Someone had to remind me, so I'm reminding you too. Don't laugh. It is all true.

The Perks of Reaching Fifty or Being over Sixty and Heading toward Seventy

Kidnappers are not very interested in you.

In a hostage situation, you are likely to be released first.

No one expect you to run—anywhere.

People call at 9:00 p.m. and ask, "Did I wake you?"

People no longer view you as a hypochondriac.

There is nothing left to learn the hard way.

Things you buy now won't wear out.

You can eat supper at 4:00 p.m.

You can live without sex but not your glasses!

You get into heated arguments about pension plans.

You no longer think of speed limits as a challenge.

You quit trying to hold your stomach in no matter who walks into the room.

You sing along with elevator music.

Your eyes won't get much worse.

Your investment in health insurance is finally paying off.

Your joints are more accurate meteorologists than the National Weather Bureau.

Your secrets are safe with your friends because they can't remember them either.

Your supply of brain cells is finally down to manageable size.

You cannot remember who sent you this list.

And you notice these are all big print for your convenience.

Never, under any circumstances, take a sleeping pill and a laxative on the same night.

Wives Don't Forget Old Boyfriends

A husband took his wife to a disco on the weekend. There was a guy on the dance floor giving it large—breakdancing, moonwalking, back-flips—the works.

The wife turned to the husband and said, "See that guy? Twenty-five years ago, he proposed to me, and I turned him down."

Husband says, "Looks like he's still celebrating!"

The Church Organist or Better than a Flu Shot

Miss Beatrice, the church organist, was in her eighties and had never been married. She was admired for her sweetness and kindness to all. One afternoon, the pastor came to call on her, and she showed him into the quaint sitting room. She invited him to have a seat while she prepared tea.

As he sat facing her old Hammond organ, the priest noticed a cut glass bowl sitting on top of it. The bowl was filled with water, and in the bowl of water floated—of all things—a condom!

When she returned with tea and scones, they began to chat. The pastor tried to stifle his curiosity about the bowl of water and its strange floater, but soon, it got the better of him and he could no longer resist.

"Miss Beatrice," he said, "I wonder if you could tell me about this?" Pointing to the bowl, he said.

"Oh yes," she replied, "Isn't it wonderful? I was walking through the park a few months ago, and I found this little package on the ground. The directions said to place it on the organ, keep it wet, and that it would prevent the spread of disease. Do you know I have not had the flu all winter?"

This Is a Warning: Never Force Children to Pray

At dinner, a little boy was forced to lead the family into prayer…

Little boy: But I do not know how to pray.

Dad: Just pray for your family members, friends, neighbors, the poor, etc.

Little boy: Dear Lord. Thank you for our visitors and their children who finished all my cookies and ice cream. Bless them so they won't come again. Forgive our neighbor's son, who removed my sister's clothes and wrestled with her on her bed. This coming Christmas, please send clothes for those poor naked ladies on my daddy's Blackberry and provide shelter for the homeless men who use Mom's room when Daddy is at work. Amen.

Headlines in Newspapers

Something went wrong in jet plane crash, expert says
Police begin campaign to run down jaywalkers
Panda mating fails; veterinarian takes over
Miners refuse to work after death
Was dims hope for peace?
If strike isn't settled quickly, it may last a while
Cold wave lined to temperatures
Red tape holds up bridge construction
Man struck by lightning faces battery charge
New study of obesity looks for larger test group
Astronaut takes blame for gas in spacecraft
Local high school dropouts cut in half
Couple slain; police suspect homicide
Hospitals are sued by seven foot doctors
Da-dah—and the winner is…
Typhoon rips through cemetery. Hundreds dead.

A Well-Planned Retirement

Outside England's Bristol Zoo, there is a parking lot for one hundred and fifty cars and eight busses. For twenty-five years, its parking fees were managed by a very pleasant attendant. The fees were L1 for cars ($1.90) and L5 for busses (about $9.00)

Then, one day, after twenty-five solid years of never missing a day of work, he just did not show up. So the zoo management called the city council and asked it to send them another parking agent.

The council did some research and replied that the parking lot was the zoo's responsibility. The zoo advised the council that the attendant was a city employee. The city council responded that the lot attendant had never been on the city payroll.

Meanwhile, sitting in his villa somewhere on the coast of Spain (or some such scenario) is a man who'd apparently had a ticket machine installed completely on his own; and then had simply begun to show up every day, commencing to collect and keep the parking fees, estimated at $ 760.00 per day—for twenty-five years.

Assuming seven days a week, this amounts to over 9.5 million dollars!

And no one knows his name.

The IRS Agent

At the end of the tax year, the IRS office sent an inspector to audit the books of a local hospital. While the IRS agent was checking the books, he turned to the CFO of the hospital and said, "I notice you buy a lot of bandages. What do you do with the end of the roll when there's too little to be of any use?"

"Good question," noted the CFO. "We save them up and send them back to the bandage company, and every now and then, they send us a free box of bandages."

"Oh," replied the auditor, somewhat disappointed that his unusual question had a practical answer. But on he went, in his obnoxious way, "What about these plaster purchases? What do you do with what's left over after setting a cast for a patient."

"Ah yes," replied the CFO, realizing that the inspector was trying to trap him with and unanswerable question. "We save it and send it back to the manufacturer, and every now and then, they send us a free package of plaster."

"I see," replied the auditor, thinking hard about how he could fluster the know-it-all CFO. "Well," he went on, "what do you do with all the leftover foreskins from the circumcisions you perform?"

"Here, too, we do not waste," answered the CFO. "What we do is save all the little foreskins and send them to the IRS office, and about once a year, they send us a complete dick."

The Nudist Colony

A man moves into a nudist colony. He receives a letter from his grandmother, asking him to send her a current photo of himself in his new location.

Too embarrassed to let her know that he lives in a nudist colony, he cuts a photo in half and mails it.

The next day he discovered that he had accidently sent the bottom half of the photo. He's really worried but then remembers how bad his grandmother's eyesight is and hopes she won't notice.

A few weeks later, he received a letter from his grandmother.

It said, "Thank you for the picture. Change your hairstyle. It makes your nose look too short. Love, Grandma."

How Past Patriots Astutely Handled Negative Comments about America

JFK's secretary of state, Dean Rusk, was in France in the early sixties when Charles DeGaulle decided to pull out of NATO. DeGaulle said he wanted all U.S. military out of France as soon as possible.

Rusk responded, "Does that include those who are buried here?" DeGaulle did not respond.

When in England, at a fairly large conference, Colin Powell was asked by the archbishop of Canterbury if our plans for Iraq were just an example of "empire building" by George Bush.

He answered by saying, "Over the years, the United States has sent many of its fine young men and women into great peril to fight for freedom beyond our borders. The only amount of land we have ever asked for in return is enough to bury those that did not return."

There was a conference in France where a number of international engineers were taking part, including French and American. During a break, one of the French engineers came back into the room, saying, "Have you heard the latest dumb stunt Bush has done? He has sent an aircraft carrier to Indonesia to help the tsunami victims. What does he intend to do, bomb them?"

A Boeing engineer stood up and replied quietly, "Our carriers have three hospitals on board that can treat several hundred people. They are nuclear powered and can supply emergency electrical power to shore facilities. They have three cafeterias with the capacity to feed five thousand people three meals a day. They can produce several thousand gallons of fresh water from sea water each day, and they carry half a dozen helicopters for use in transporting victims and injured to and from their flight deck. We have eleven such ships. How many does France have?"

An Old Veteran

Robert Whiting, an elderly gentleman of eighty-three, arrived in Paris by plane. At French Customs, he took a few minutes to locate his passport in his carry-on.

"You have been to France before, monsieur?" the customs officer asked sarcastically.

Mr. Whiting admitted to being to France before.

"Then you should know enough to have your passport ready."

The American said, "The last time I was here, I didn't have to show it."

"Impossible. Americans always have to show their passports on arrival in France!"

The American senior gave the Frenchman a long hard look. Then he quietly explained, "Well, when I came ashore at Omaha Beach on D-Day in 1944 to help liberate this country, I couldn't find a single Frenchman to show a passport to."

Live by Design,

Love by Nature,

and

Laugh Out Loud!

by

Robert J. Denise

The Italians

Do you know why most men from Italy are named Tony? On the boat over to America, they put a sticker on them that said "TO NY," which meant To New York.

You know you are Italian when you can bench press 325 pounds, shave twice a day, and still cry when your mother yells at you.

You carry your lunch in a produce bag because you can't fit two cappicola sandwiches, four oranges, two bananas, and prizzelles unto a regular lunch bag.

Your mechanic, plumber, electrician, accountant, travel agent, and lawyer are all your cousins.

You are on a first name basis with at least eight banquet hall owners.

You only get one good shave from a disposable razor.

If someone in your family grows beyond five feet nine inches, it is presumed your mother had an affair.

There were more than twenty-eight people in your bridal party.

You netted more than fifty thousand dollars on your first communion.

You really, really know you are Italian when your grandfather had a fig tree.

Your mom's meatballs are the best.

When your mom would discipline you with the spaghetti spoon, if she could catch you, or you had a shoe thrown at you.

Clear plastic covers on all the furniture.

You know how to pronounce *manicotti* or *mozzarella*.

You fight over whether it is called sauce or gravy.

You've called someone a "mama Luke," and you understand "bada bing."

Italians do not care about cholesterol.

Turkey is served on Thanksgiving after the manicotti, gnocchi, lasagna, and minestrone or shcarole soup.

If anyone *ever* says *escaole*, slap 'em in the face—it is *shcarole*.

The Amazing Human Body

It takes your food seven seconds to get from your mouth to your stomach.

One human hair can support 6.6 pounds.

The average man's penis is two times the length of his thumb.

Human thighbones are stronger than concrete.

A woman's heart beats faster than a man's.

There are about one trillion bacteria on each of your feet.

Women blink twice as often as men.

The average person's skin weighs twice as much as the brain.

Your body uses three hundred muscles to balance itself when you are standing still.

If saliva cannot dissolve something, you cannot taste it.

Women will be finished reading this by now. Men are still busy checking out their thumbs.

Only in America

Only in America do drugstores make the sick walk all the way to the back of the store to get their prescriptions while healthy people can buy cigarettes at the front.

Only in America do people order double cheeseburgers, large fries, and a diet Coke.

Only in America do banks leave both doors open, and then chain the pens to the counters.

Only in America do we leave cars worth thousands of dollars in the driveway and put our worthless junk in the garage.

Only in America do we buy hot fogs in packages of ten, and buns in packages of eight.

Only in America do we use the word *politics* to describe the process so well. *Poli* in Latin meaning "many," and *tics*, meaning "bloodsucking creatures."

Only in America do we have drive up ATMs with Braille lettering.

Ever Wonder

Why the sun lightens our hair, but darkens our skin?
Why can't women put mascara on with their mouth closed?
Why don't you ever see the headline, "Psychic Wins Lottery"?
Why is abbreviated such a long word?
Why is the time of day with the slowest traffic called *rush hour*?
Why didn't Noah swat those two mosquitoes?
Why do they sterilize the needle for lethal injections?
Why isn't there mouse-flavored cat food?
If flying is so safe, why do they call the airport the terminal?
If *con* is the opposite of *pro*, is *congress* the opposite of *progress*?

A New York Love Story

A beautiful young New York woman was so depressed that she decided to end her life by throwing herself into the ocean. But just before she could throw herself from the docks, a handsome young man stopped her.

"You have so much to live for," said the man. "Look, I am a sailor, and we are off to Europe tomorrow, and I can stow you away on my ship. I'll take care of you, bring you food every day, and keep you happy."

With nothing to lose, and since she had always wanted to go to Europe, the woman accepted.

That night, the sailor brought her aboard and hid her in a lifeboat. From then on, every night, he would bring her three sandwiches and make love to her until dawn.

Three weeks later, during a routine inspection, she was discovered by the captain.

"What are you doing here?" he asked.

"I have an arrangement with one of your sailors," she replied. "He brings me food every night, and I get a free trip to Europe! Plus, he's screwing me every night."

"He certainly is," replied the captain.

"This is the Staten Island ferry."

The *W*in Christmas

Unknown Author

Each Christmas, I vowed to make Christmas a calm and peaceful experience. I had cut back on nonessential obligations—extensive card writing, endless baking, decorating, and even overspending. Yet still, I found myself exhausted, unable to appreciate the precious family moments—the true meaning of Christmas.

My son Edward was in kindergarten that year. It was an exciting season for a six-year-old. For weeks, he'd been memorizing songs for his school's winter pageant.

I did not have the heart to tell him I'd be working the night of the production. Unwilling to miss his shining moment, I spoke with his teacher. She assured me there'd be a dress rehearsal the morning of the presentation. All parents unable to attend that evening were welcome to come then. Fortunately, Edward seemed happy with the compromise.

So the morning of the dress rehearsal, I filed in ten minutes early, found a spot on the cafeteria floor, and sat down. As I waited, the students were led into the room. Each class, accompanied by their teacher, sat cross-legged on the floor. Then, each group, one by one, rose to perform their song.

Because the public school system had long stopped referring to the holiday as Christmas, I did not expect anything other than fun, commercial entertainment, songs of reindeer, Santa Claus, snowflakes, and good cheer. So when my son's class rose to sing "Christmas Love," I was slightly taken back by its bold title.

Edward was aglow, as were all of his classmates, adorned in fuzzy mittens, red sweaters, and bright snowcaps upon their heads. Those in the front row center stage held up large letters, one by one, to spell out the title of the song. As the class would sing *C* is for Christmas, a child would hold up the letter *C*. Then, *H* is for happy, and on and on, until each child holding up his portion had presented the complete message, "Christmas Love."

The performance was going smoothly until suddenly, we noticed her; a small quiet girl in the front row holding the letter *M* upside down. She was totally unaware that her letter *M* appeared as a *W*.

The audience of first through sixth graders snickered at the little one's mistake. But she had no idea they were laughing at her, so she stood tall, proudly holding her *W*. Although many teachers tried to shush the children, the laughter continued until the last letter was raised, and we all saw it together. A hush came over the audience, and eyes began to widen. In that instant, we understood the reason we were there, why we celebrated the holiday in the first place, why even in the chaos, there was a clear purpose for our festivities.

For when the last letter was held high, the message read loud and clear: C H R I S T W A S L O V E.

Best-Ever Senior Citizen Joke

A little silver-haired lady calls her neighbor and says, "Please come over here and help me. I have a killer jigsaw puzzle. And I can't figure out how to get started."

Her neighbor asks, "What is it supposed to be when it's finished?"

The little silver-haired lady says, "According to the picture on the box, it's a rooster."

Her neighbor decides to go over and help with the puzzle.

She lets him in and shows him where she has the puzzle spread all over the table. He studies the pieces for a moment, then looks at the box, then turns to her and says, "First of all, no matter what we do, we're not going to be able to assemble these pieces into anything resembling a rooster."

He takes her hand and says, "Secondly, I want you to relax. Let's have a nice cup of tea." And then, he said with a deep sigh, "Let's put all the corn flakes back in the box."

God help us all!

Ten Rules for an Educator

1. Be great and have fun, this is what you worked for. It's a great life.
2. Your educational day does not begin and end; it continues.
3. Accept the fact that nobody really appreciates you in government. If they did, we would not have vouchers and charter/private schools that siphon money away from your students!
4. You challenge every belief you have before your students do.
5. Model everything.
6. Be open and receptive to change, even if you think it is junk because this is the way.
7. Do not ask, demand perfection from your students and see what you get. I will bet it is better than what you may have asked for!
8. Do not send students to the office. Handle it yourself because your people skills will improve. Oh, did I mention, your discussions with parents will help you as a teacher. Invite them to class and see the difference.
9. Do not be afraid of anyone or anything!
10. Expect the unexpected. Kids protect kids, not teachers.
11. Every day, every minute, and every second is different, that is what makes being a teacher so great!
12. If you want a student to be your friend, it is a prescription for failure, big time. Buy a dog.
13. Don't blame other for student shortcomings, blame yourself! You organize, you organize, you present, you answer

questions you did not understand "how to" motivate your students. Get to know them better.

14. Identify students you consider troubled. Read their files, talk to the student and set classroom parameters, the counselor, the parent, find out what he/she has for interests and work them into your class and then positively reinforce that student by working questions into your plan that involve that student.

15. There will be bumps along the way. Do not show emotion. Do not be confrontational.

H. L. Mencken (born 1880; died 1956) was a journalist, satirist, critic, and a Democrat. He wrote this editorial while working for the *Baltimore Evening Sun*. It appeared in the July 26, 1920, edition.

"As democracy is perfected, the office of the president represents, more and more closely, the inner soul of the people. On some great and glorious days, the plain folks of the land will reach their heart's desire at last and the White House will be occupied by a downright fool and complete narcissistic moron."

Saint Peter

Saint Peter is sitting at the Pearly Gates when two guys wearing dark hoodies and sagging pants arrive. Saint Peter looked out through the gates and said, "Wait here. I'll be right back." Saint Peter goes over to God's chambers and tells him who is waiting for entrance.

God says to Peter, "How many times do I have to tell you? You can't be judgmental here! This is heaven. All are loved. All are brothers. Go back and let them in!"

Saint Peter goes back to the gates, looks around, and lets out a heavy sigh. He returns to God's chambers and says, "Well, they're gone."

"The guys wearing hoodies?" asked God.

"No…the Pearly Gates."

A Chicken Farmer

A chicken farmer went to a local bar. He sat next to a woman and ordered champagne.

The woman said, "How strange. I just ordered a glass of champagne."

"What a coincidence," said the farmer, who added, "it is a special day for me. I am celebrating."

"It is a special day for me too, I am also celebrating!" said the woman.

"What a coincidence," said the farmer.

While they toasted, the man asked, "What are you celebrating?"

"My husband and I have been trying to have a child for years, and today, my gynecologist told me that I was pregnant."

"What a coincidence!" said the farmer. "I am a chicken farmer, and for many years, all my hens were infertile, but now they are all set to lay fertilized eggs."

"This is awesome," said the woman. "What did you do for your chickens to become fertile?"

"I used a different rooster," he said.

You've probably guessed right.

The woman smiled and said, "What a coincidence."

From the Shelter of My Mind, Through the Window of My Eyes

My eyes have seen many injustices in my lifetime that have always left me thinking, why should I, a middle-class slug, lead and exemplary life when people who have the public trust always seem to be in it for themselves? So I made a list of the things that have made me discouraged:

May we start with the president, who talks a good game, but in the last five years plus, what has he and his staffers delivered to alleviate a budget crisis, monetary crisis—oh and lest we forget no new jobs with benefits. It is all takeaways. Man up and do your job!

Oh, and by the way, the Congress, whom we elected to do our bidding in Washington and who are supposed to be helpful cannot even agree to compromise (including the president). You should all be goddammed ashamed of the job the people sent you to Washington to accomplish. Remember it is you who are eliminating jobs, eliminating health benefits, and giving the people nothing. That is correct—nothing in return to hope for except an eighteen-trillion-dollar deficit.

Where is the America I grew up in? It is lost in socialistic bullshit and a trickle-up poverty that threatens to bankrupt our country. Can caves be far from reality for us also?

Go ahead, print more money, devalue the dollar quicker, and tell us it is just the economy. Don't you realize if you ran your businesses like this, you would have a brown box with your mementos and security guards taking you to the curb? Now you can live like the rest of us, and you should.

Oh, Obamacare. How many of you read what you voted on? Did you really vote to give the president, his family, and your family an exemption from it? How high above the law do you want to be?

We were never in a recession. We were and are possibly in a depression now. Did it ever occur to you that the answer to moving America forward was found in history and putting people back to work just as Franklin Delano Roosevelt did? Why not put out of work plumbers, construction workers, etc. to work building affordable housing for the people who cannot afford it, and giving them a shot at life?

Why was there only one man who went to jail for a Ponzi scheme, but no one in banking, the real estate market, or Wall Street investors went to jail?

Why can't normal people run the government? They have the most to lose and the least to earn because CEOs need their sixteen-million-dollar payoffs for screwing the American people in the name of stockholders profits.

Why can't we build more refineries? Too much oil? Lower price? Fish, ducks, and assorted other animals will be adversely affected they say, or maybe BP will do the drilling, or there will be another Exxon Valdez. $3.65–700 for an industry that all charges every person the same amount. Why have the Sherman Anti-Trust Act on the books if we do not use it?

Why does it cost so much for air tickets, so much for trains, so much for clothing—because oil is part of their product?

Wait, saved the best for last. All you senior citizens, when Obamacare kicks in, you are in a heck of a lot of trouble. Ever notice that every time the government gets involved in your life, your life gets screwed up? Wait.

About the Author

The author lives in a small, rural community in Massachusetts. The author is a life-long educator and sports enthusiast, he is a coach, a teacher, a football, basketball, and a baseball coach at the high school level and a football official at the college level. He was selected to be an equipment manager for the 1996 Atlanta Olympic Games.

The inspiration this first work came from a quote he heard and it just grew and grew. It was always a goal to produce a book that had a very good pace and reached out the reader and made he/she pause and think after reading the quote or the story.

This is a perfect think tank for any teacher at any level of education as well individuals who want to be entertained and experience various human emotions as they read this volume

CPSIA information can be obtained
at www.ICGtesting.com
Printed in the USA
BVHW081540050321
601818BV00001B/120

9 781634 175562